LEADERSHIP

Growing and Sustaining
A Smaller Organization

ROBERT FOLLETT

LEADERSHIP: Growing and Sustaining a Smaller Organization

ISBN: 0-931712-30-0

Published by
Alpine Guild, Inc.
P.O. Box 4848, Dillon, CO 80435
www.alpineguild.com

Printed in the United States of America. First printing 2012.

The web site for this book is www.leadershiptasks.com

INTRODUCTION

Welcome! This book is aimed at growing and sustaining a smaller organization – your organization. The time you spend with this book should help you make your organization more successful.

The book was written to provide a structured sequence of thinking tasks, then a sequence of doing tasks. These tasks, well done, will build success.

The leadership of a smaller organization is demanding. Usually the leader is involved with day-to-day management and often with front-line activities. This book is focused on *leadership*, the critical tasks, activities, and factors that are essential for the success of your organization.

I want you to have a successful career as a leader. This book aims to help you reach that goal.

In a way this book began in a restaurant. My wife and I were eating when a young man came over to the table.

"I've seen your picture in the paper. I know you have led many organizations. Why don't you write a book to help younger leaders like me. I am sure you would have lots of good advice."

When he went back to his table my mind was churning.

I thought about all the dumb mistakes I had made, the projects that had failed. But then I remembered the successes, too. From my long experience as a leader I thought that I might have something useful to say to other leaders.

My wife ended my reverie. "Why not?" she said. "You have already written several books. You ought to be able to help other leaders with all your experience."

And so this book began. First, with a lot of thought, then with writing and rewriting. And now you have the finished product in your hands. I hope it will provide ideas and activities that will help to grow and sustain your organization, in both good times and bad times.

You will find that this book expects you to do more than just read.

You can read through the book easily in one sitting. But its benefits can only come from spending time and effort to undertake the sequence of leadership tasks that the book sets forth.

The book is divided into several sections. The first deals with *Thinking Tasks*. The second section deals with *Doing Tasks*. These tasks are essential to organizational success.

The purpose of this book is to guide you through the thinking and doing tasks so your organization can achieve maximum success. This book sets out a structured process that will make your success much more likely. It is a process I developed out of much work as a leader of several organizations, both for-profit and not-for profit.

A friend who consults with small businesses told me this: "I have never worked with any business leader who had a written plan whose organization failed. Good planning leads to success."

I want you to lead an organization that will not fail. I want you to achieve success.

You may be the CEO of a sizeable organization or of a smaller one. Or you might be the head of the governing board of an organization.

This book will be of benefit to you if you exercise leadership in your organization.

Whatever the size of the organization you lead, you will find much to help you be a more effective leader.

As the title indicates, this book is aimed at smaller organizations. Large organizations that have whole departments dedicated to planning, that can hire expensive consultants, that have many layers of management – these are not the organizations this book was written for.

Leaders of large organizations should find benefits in the book. Start-up entrepreneurs should get value from the book. But organizations that fall between these extremes are the focus of this book.

How small is smaller? If you pretty well know all of the names and faces of the people in your organization, then it fits the definition of smaller for this book.

Of course, most organizations hope to grow to be large. This book will be a valuable guide to getting there.

Your organization might be a business aiming to make a profit. Or it might be a not-for-profit organization. But whatever kind of organization, it must consistently have more money coming in than going out.

Your organization might be a retail store, an internet provider, a wholesaler, a manufacturer, or any other kind of for-profit business set up by investors hoping to make a profit.

Or your organization might be an orchestra, museum, social service agency, or medical provider funded by governments, foundations, client payments, and donor gifts. Those putting money into these kinds of organizations expect that its clients will gain benefits.

People involved with either for-profit or not-for-profit businesses expect results. This book is aimed at making good results more likely. It aims to help you build a sustainable organization and one that can grow successfully.

Leader and *manager* are sometimes words used interchangeably. But they are not the same. Leaders are responsible for setting goals, establishing values, and seeing that the organization achieves long-term success. Managers are responsible for the day-to-day activities that accomplish the goals.

In smaller organizations the leader is also often a manager. And may be doing some of the basic work of the organization as well. But this book is aimed at your success as a *leader*.

Leaders, much research has shown, do not have a specific set of personality characteristics. Leaders are not born, they are created when they assume leadership responsibility.

This responsibility does not mean the leader has to single-handedly meet the challenges the organization faces. Rather the leader must enlist others involved with the organization to meet and solve challenges.

The leader needs to clearly define the issues and objectives. The leader needs to assure coordination and cooperation between those whose work is needed.

You are a leader if you have a leadership position.

This book might be used by one person. But better yet, it should be the basis for a team effort. When a team addresses the issues, more brainpower is brought to bear. An individual can seldom be as smart as a group. Marshal all the brainpower you can so that your organization effectively uses the ideas in this book to guide the organization to long-term success.

This book often outlines tasks for "the leader" or for "you." I did not intend that these tasks should always be done just by one person. In most cases, the tasks will produce better outcomes when more than one person – a team – is involved. So when the book says "you" be thinking of the team. But you must lead the team.

Of course there are some tasks that only the leader can do. There are many that are far better done by a team. And then there are some that you may want to delegate to others. Your supervisors can head up some of the activities. But as the leader you must always be sure that the outcomes are appropriate and effective for your organization.

This book asks you to undertake a sequential set of thinking tasks. Thinking, especially thinking about the uncertain future, is hard work. But it is very important work.

All too many leaders want to leap in, get started doing something. But if they haven't thought out what to do, how to do it, when to do it, they often end up with lots of action and little movement.

Most of us depend most of the time on intuition, hunches, feelings, and other non-rigorous (and often unconscious) ways of making decisions. This works for the trivial decisions we make every day. And these decisions come easily.

But decisions about your organization, especially decisions that impact the future, need to be made much more carefully, with much more conscious thought. This takes time and effort.

Reacting with intuition, hunches, thoughts that come quickly and easily to mind is not difficult. Thinking carefully about issues is hard work. But it is this hard work of conscious thought that will produce success for your organization.

This book is aimed at helping you move your organization forward to lasting success. That's why the first section is concerned with thinking carefully about your business and writing down your conclusions – conclusions that will form the basis for the doing actions that will then be taken.

This book begins with two main sections. The first, *Thinking Tasks,* starts by asking you to come up with definitions – what products and services you offer, who your customers or clients are, what benefits your customers or clients expect from you, what the organization's core competencies are, and what you and others in your organization want.

But of course, you know all that. Or do you? If you haven't thought about these things and written down your conclusions, it is easy to get off track. This chapter on definitions may be the most important one in the book.

Once you have come up with carefully-thought-out definitions, the next thinking task is creating a mission statement. This will become a public document, to be shared with your customers or clients, your investors or donors, lenders, suppliers, community leaders, and of course, employees. A mission statement that accurately and positively characterizes your organization will take time and effort to construct. A good mission statement should attract both people and money to your organization.

All organizations have values. But often they are values that haven't been thought through and often they do not support the mission. The values that will guide you and your staff to right actions that support the mission need to be articulated. You need to make sure all employees know these values. Good values, consistently applied, are critical to long-term success for your organization.

Then comes thinking through a vision. What do you want your organization to look like in five years? You will need to think through your hopes and dreams for the future. The vision sets goals for the future. A good vision should have inspiring goals but also be attainable, with hard work.

But you will also need to think about the potential barriers that might need to be overcome to achieve the vision. There will be unexpected surprises and problems. You need to think about what they might be and how you would respond. This chapter suggests a number of possible barriers that might arise.

Next is the strategic plan. This is the five-year plan that will accomplish the vision for the organization. The strategic plan must consider where the money will come from and what it will be spent on – a cash flow plan that ensures that financial troubles will not derail the organization. (The book contains a sample cash flow planning budget that will help you create your own.) There also needs to be a five-year organizational and staffing plan.

Once there is a strategic plan, then you can work on the annual budget. This is the plan for the coming year that will accomplish the first year of the strategic plan. The budget will need a cash flow plan for the year that ensures that the organization will have the financial resources needed for its success.

Completing these thinking tasks will demand time and effort. What is the payoff for the expenditure of this time and effort?

I have found over many years that the payoff is a more successful organization, an organization with much sharper focus, an organization far better prepared to deal with unexpected challenges as well as opportunities. When an organization grows and sustains itself successfully, then the organization's leader is successful. I want you to be successful so I encourage you to give the time and effort that these tasks require.

With these thinking tasks completed, and the results of the thinking put on paper as an ongoing road map and guide, you will be ready for the second section of the book.

This section is concerned with *Doing Tasks.* These are the main tasks that must be done to accomplish the mission, the vision, and the plans that have been created.

The first doing task is staffing. How do you go about getting the staff you need to accomplish your goals? Staffing includes writing job descriptions, recruiting candidates, interviewing, hiring – and termination, if a staffing choice turns out to be a bad fit.

You may already have all the staff you need. But if you are to grow, you will probably need additional staff. This chapter will help.

Staffing may be handled by others in the organization, but the leader of a smaller organization must be closely involved. Getting the right people into the organization is a primary component of success. The leader must always be focused on getting the right people on the staff.

Some organizations rush to fill vacancies. This often leads to getting the wrong person. Success for the organization is more likely when time is taken to find and hire the right person.

This chapter of staffing also includes a section on using outside resources (rather than hiring.)

Once a person has been hired they must be trained. The next chapter covers training as well as ongoing coaching.

Another very important part of building a successful team is enculturation – helping a new employee fit into your organization's culture. There is a chapter on this important topic.

The next doing task for a leader is directing. This means seeing that the staff takes those actions that will move the organization forward to meet its mission, vision, and plans. Self-direction by employees is by far the best kind of direction. What needs to be done to lead employees to take responsibility for their own self-direction? This chapter sets out important actions a leader must take.

As an organization grows, responsibility and authority must be delegated to others so the leader has the time for the key leadership tasks. There is a section on how to delegate effectively.

Controlling is the next doing task. This means regularly assessing what is happening, comparing the actual results to the planned results, and taking the actions needed to correct activities that are not performing as planned. (Or revising the plans to meet changed conditions that could not be anticipated.) The walk-around is an important aspect of controlling covered in this chapter.

The Doing section ends with a diagram of the great circle – the leadership mandala. This shows how each leadership task flows into the next, coming back to the starting point as the great circle turns. It is helpful to see these tasks as sequential, one leading to the next in a circle.

In smaller organizations, the leader is often involved in many of the daily activities. The leader is often a manager and is often a doer. The leader may act as a worker – creating products, delivering services, marketing and selling, and so on.

In my career, I have swept the floor and packed the products for shipment. I often worked face-to-face with customers. I have written advertising copy. But these were not leadership activities. The leader must be clear about the difference between the leadership role and other roles.

Ultimately, the leader bears the responsibility for the organization's success or failure. Sweeping floors, packing shipments, working with customers or clients, writing copy is not the way to assume that responsibility. A leader must never let the day-to-day requirements of the operation obscure the ultimate responsibility. Often people designated as leaders are so busy tending to the daily crisis that they ignore the key thinking and doing tasks that only they can effectively perform. Such people are not really leading.

After these two important sections on Thinking and Doing, there is a chapter on SWOT analysis. This is a valuable team process in which the organization analyzes its *Strengths* and *Weaknesses*, its *Opportunities* and *Threats*. This analysis often requires going back to the thinking tasks to redo them in light of the conclusions reached in the SWOT analysis.

Then there is a chapter on costs vs. benefits. This recommends that leaders to do careful cost-benefit analysis for any proposed project or investment that would significantly impact the organization. Replacing hunches, intuition, and good feelings with sound analysis will prevent many disasters. The analysis of any project for the future needs to consider the worst-case scenario as well as the expected outcome. Often enough, it is the worst case – the black swan – that actually happens.

The best team wins! This chapter deals with the team – how the leader needs to act in order to strengthen the team. There are several important leadership activities that help build a successful team. And a successful team will build a successful organization.

Most leaders work for, with, or on a board. This chapter outlines key board responsibilities. The leader needs to be sure that the board meets those responsibilities. An effective working relationship with the board is critical for leaders.

Then the book sets forth some of the key ideas that I have acquired over many years as a leader of both for-profit and not-for-profit organizations. These are ideas condensed into a single sentence. They are axioms, or maxims, or principles that experience has etched into my mind and that have been both guideposts and warnings for me.

The book then ends with a summary of all that has been covered.

The Appendix follows. It shows the cash flow planning for a mythical company, Acme Widgets. If your organization has not done cash flow planning, this Appendix will provide much help. For any organization, having more cash coming in than is going out is essential for survival. Cash flow planning helps to make that happen.

And finally, Acknowledgments – a recognition of those who have helped to make this book far better than I could have done on my own.

When you have worked your way through this book, I hope you will have gained new and necessary leadership tools for sustaining and growing a successful organization.

The greatest part of this book deals with the thinking that a leader needs to do. Thinking about the various aspects of the organization and its future takes time and effort. Most leaders of smaller organizations are heavily involved in day-to-day activities. They are often the principal creators, marketers, even deliverers of the organization's products or services. There is little time, they believe, to do all of the planning this book sets forth.

But without planning for the future, organizations all too often fail. They end up going around in circles, doing what they have been doing until the lack of planning makes them obsolete, unneeded, no longer viable in changing environments. All too often they run out of cash because they haven't planned.

I don't want you and your organization to end up like that. You must find the time and the energy to do the *thinking* that will ensure your organization's long-term success. And remember, the more brains focused on the thinking tasks, the better the results will be.

Make this book a *work*book where you (and your team, if you have one) spend time and effort to tackle tough questions and come up with useful answers. From the time and effort you spend, I am confident that you and your organization will gain much greater success.

So go to it!

SECTION ONE: THINKING TASKS

Successful leadership begins with thinking. Thinking comes before doing. The first thinking task is to clarify – and then write down – basic definitions for your organization. Other thinking tasks follow from these definitions.

If your organization has been in business for a long time you may believe all this thinking is unnecessary. You already know what your business is about. But I am sure you will find it very worthwhile to spend time on these tasks. They will help you clarify aspects of your business that you may not have given careful thought to.

One of my failures was to grab hold of a great idea and plunge in to create what I expected to be a very successful business. But I didn't do the thinking tasks that follow in this section.

The idea was great but there were a number of hurdles to clear before it could be turned into a successful business. I soon found that some of these hurdles were too high for us. We had come up with a great idea that the market was not yet ready to buy into.

So this business failed. But some years later, conditions had changed, the hurdles had been lowered. Other companies took our idea and grew successful businesses.

Had I done the thinking tasks outlined below, I can now see that the implementation of the idea could have been delayed until it could be successful.

An old Pennsylvania Dutch saying goes, "Too soon old, too late smart." Leaders who do the thinking this book proposes can avoid having this rueful saying applied to them.

18

A. <u>THE FIRST TASK – DEFINITIONS</u>

Whether yours is a long-established organization or a brand-new one, giving careful thought and attention to the definitions below will provide immediate as well as long-term benefits. These definitions will be a continuing help to your organization. The definitions will provide a sharper focus and more success.

The first three definitions are interrelated. I recommend that you consider all three before coming up with final definitions. Perhaps the best way to proceed is to put down tentative definitions. Then come back and rework the definitions in light of what you have thought through for each one. Like many other tasks outlined in this handbook, a team effort will produce more valuable results.

<u>Define your product or service</u>.

What product or service does your organization provide?

That seems simple. A restaurant owner might say, "Our product is food." But perhaps the restaurant is really providing an experience, an ambiance centered around food and wine. Or perhaps its product is food but quick service is really what it offers that customers value. Restaurants are among the businesses that fail most frequently. Perhaps it is because they haven't thought through what they are really selling.

I published textbooks at one period in my life. Some people thought our product was the print on paper, the physical book. But our real product was the learning provided by the textbook.

Consultants usually charge by the hour. But what is the product or service they are selling? It certainly isn't time. I don't even believe they are selling advice. What the client is *buying* is solutions to problems. Successful consultants sell solutions, not time or advice.

If you are a social service agency, you need to think carefully about the service you provide. Perhaps you counsel single mothers. Is your service the act of counseling or is it the result that single mothers obtain from the counseling?

Railroads might well have gone into the trucking and air freight businesses if they had defined their product/service as the delivery of goods over long distances. Instead they defined their product or service in terms of the physical structure of their enterprise – rails, locomotives, switch yards, and so forth. That left the way open for others to develop different means of moving goods.

There are many more examples of organizations misunderstanding the product or service they provide.

You can't succeed unless you understand what product or service you are really providing to your customers or clients. If you are going to sell your product or service, you need to be clear about what it is you are selling.

I suggest that you put down what products or services come out of your organization. What is it the organization bills for?

Then put down the products or services your customers or clients expect to get from your organization. Are their expectations for value from your organization the same as what you believe you are providing? Or are they different?

It isn't what your organization provides. It is what the customers or clients expect to get from you. That leads to the next definition you must do.

Define your customers or clients.

This might be very simple. "My customers are adults who live within ten minutes of my establishment." Or it can be complicated.

For example, I once published elementary school textbooks. One customer was the child who would read the textbooks. Another customer was the educator who would choose the textbooks. Yet a third customer was the financial officer who would authorize payment for the textbooks. Understanding that there were actually three different customers for one product helped us to focus on who we were selling to, and how we could maximize our selling success.

This is often the situation. Social service agencies often have clients, referred to them by social workers, doctors, etc. They may receive payment through government contracts. Is the customer the client, the referring official, or the government agency?

I recommend that you think carefully about your customers or clients. Is there just one – a person who walks in the door or goes online, gets the product or service, and pays for it? That is common in retail settings. Do you have more than one customer or client? This is common in many other areas of business.

Write down who uses your product or service. Then write down who takes the delivery of your products or services. Write down who refers the customers or clients or who makes the decision to purchase, if this is someone different. Then write down who actually approves or makes the payment, if that is yet another person. (I think of this as *user, chooser, payer.*They may be the same individual. But often they are not.)

Then you can think about which of these persons needs your most concentrated marketing effort. Is it all of them? Or will only one person make the decision that results in action? Defining your customers or clients may open your eyes to new ways to increase the success of your organization.

If you haven't clearly defined who your customers or clients are, you will not be successful. Once you are clear on who your customers or clients are, then you can work out the best ways to tell them (advertising, promotion, publicity) about the product or service you offer.

In the case of elementary school textbooks, the primary customers are the educators who make the choice. But that choice is made on the basis of the learning that the students will get. And if the textbooks are too expensive, the financial officer will veto a purchase. The primary marketing is to the educators who make the choice. But the other customers must always be kept in mind.

Thinking through a definition of the customers or clients will help you to better understand exactly what it is about your product or service that the customer or client wants. Do they want the physical product or do they really want a benefit that having the physical product provides? Do they want your service or is it the want that the service fulfills that the client really seeks.

If you are selling a product or service that is narrowly defined in your terms, but that does not address the concerns of the customer or client, you will not be as successful as you could be.

Perhaps if you thought about the actual benefits that you are providing to customers or clients, you might see your operations in a completely different way. Those benefits might be valuable to a much broader audience than you currently target. Or the audience you have defined might be much more eager to come to you if they felt that the benefits your organization provided really met their wants.

There are other things you need to consider. Some organizations have only a single customer. This is often the case with a small company supplying a giant corporation or government agency. This can be a very good arrangement. But it is also highly risky. If another company comes along with a better product or a cheaper product, you may suddenly have no customer. A company with a single customer needs to spend much time and effort seeing to it that the product and its cost are always going to be able to fend off competitors. Or else the company needs to find ways to broaden its customer base.

Not-for-profit organizations also may have only one customer. They may serve many clients, but if the payment comes from a single government agency or foundation, that payer could go away almost overnight. Then what would the organization do? Thinking about clients and customers requires thinking about worst-case scenarios.

There is yet another aspect to think about. How many customers or clients are there that your organization can effectively serve?

A restaurant cannot expect to draw customers from far away. The customer base is likely to be located within an easy driving distance, as well as defined by age, income, and so on.

Your organization's customer/client base may be limited by geography or by interest in your product or service, or by availability of funds, or by other limitations.

You should write down the maximum number of customers or clients you can reasonably hope to serve with the products or services you provide. Then determine how much revenue each customer or client might reasonably generate. This will give you the maximum revenue that you can expect from the operations of your organization as you have currently defined them.

That maximum revenue will tell you how large your organization can hope to grow – unless it expands its products or services, or expands its customer/client base.

If you find this maximum puts a too tight limit on how large the organization can grow, you have some more thinking tasks to tackle.

I work with a fine summer science camp. The camp has only so many beds. The summer season only encompasses so many weeks. There is an acceptable price range for summer camps. Too high and parents won't spend to send their children. So the number of beds, times the number of days, times the camp fee (broken down to a daily figure) gives the maximum potential revenues this camp can expect. Those maximum revenues set a top limit on all of the expenses if the camp is to be financially viable. To increase the camp's maximum revenue potential, it is clear that more beds will be needed to accommodate more campers.

What is your organization's current maximum potential?

The next section asks for another critical definition.

Define what your customers or clients *want* and the *value* that you provide them.

Many organizations develop a product or service they are sure their customers need. Perhaps the customers do need it, but people buy what they *want*. That is not necessarily the same as what they need.

People in extreme poverty in Africa use extra money to buy sugary foods rather than foods with more calories. They need the calories. They want the sugar.

Sometimes advertising and promotion can convert a need into a want, a want that will activate customer response. But it is much better if you have a product or service that your customers or clients know they want. If you aren't sure what it is about the product or service you provide that customers actually want and value, you can waste time and effort in trying to create and sell something that has low value to your potential customers.

Remember, customers don't care what you put *into* a product or service. They care about what they can get *out of it*.

Finding out what your potential customers actually want, as opposed to what you may think they need, is a key part of success. Successful organizations constantly ask, probe, inquire to be sure they have a good understanding of what their customers want.

As a leader you must personally ask your customers or clients what they want. Of course, you probably won't be able to speak to every one of them. But you can't sit in your office and expect to really understand their wants. An important leadership responsibility is getting direct personal feed-back from customers or clients.

Software engineers have often created products that do everything that a software engineer can think of. They too often create software to impress their colleagues. What the customers want is a product that is immediately transparent, that requires little or no learning to be able to use, that does what the customers want it to do, without cluttering things up with excess baggage of interest only to software engineers.

24

Orchestras around the world are facing problems. Many orchestra leaders believe that audiences need to hear the great works of renowned composers. But often, the audience wants entertainment, not culture. The orchestras that understand this have changed their programming and have been able to attract more young people and a larger audience.

You can think of other examples where the creators of products or services have failed to understand and satisfy the wants of the customer.

I recommend that you write down your understanding of what your customers or clients actually want from your organization. What benefits do they hope to realize when they come to your organization? If you are not sure, you need to take steps to get as realistic answers as possible. Talk to actual or potential customers or clients. Be sure to talk to anyone in your organization who has direct contact with customers or clients. Open your ears, open your mind to find out what your organization is doing or can do to satisfy the *wants* of customers or clients.

Customers or clients cannot always articulate what they want. Much research has shown that many, perhaps most, of our decisions are guided by subconscious motives. We may not be able to articulate what we want because the want lies below our consciousness. There are a number of recent books and articles that dig into this and that suggest means to uncover the real wants of customers or clients and ways to bring those wants to the surface where they will direct action.

An effective leader is regularly meeting face-to-face with customers or clients. And then listening. Not telling, but actively listening so as to truly understand the wants of customers or clients and what it is they value most about the organization's activities.

One of the misconceptions that leads organizations astray is confusing *value* with *price*. The lowest-priced item or service may not provide the best value. If the most important benefit you are providing customers or clients is low price, you invite trouble. Perhaps a competitor will be able to come up with an even lower price. Or perhaps customers or clients are looking for results that a cheap product or service cannot provide. An emphasis on *value* should always be the first consideration. If value can be provided at a low cost, it certainly should be. But if value is sacrificed in order to cut the price, the organization is at risk.

Now that you have written down your tentative conclusions for these three definitions, you can go back to the beginning and write down your clarified and well-thought-out definitions, definitions of your product or service, of your customers or clients, and of the real wants that your organization must work to satisfy.

These definitions are going be the foundation on which the success of your organization will be built. They will keep you focused, help you avoid opportunities that seem attractive, but don't fit.

Here is another mistake I made. My company saw an opportunity to go into the indoor tennis club business. The growing numbers of young, active men and women seemed to be a market with great potential. It was, but not for us.

We didn't know anything about this business. We didn't understand what it was we were really selling. (It was not time on the tennis courts as we supposed.) We didn't have a good grasp of who the customers were. There weren't nearly as many ready to come to our courts as we had thought. What the potential customers actually wanted was different than what we thought they needed. We got into the business, couldn't make it a success, and got out at a loss. If we had gone through the thinking process that has been outlined here, we wouldn't have made that mistake.

One last word. These definitions are not cast in concrete. As external events occur, as your environment changes, as your organization comes up with innovative new ideas, you will want to reconsider the definitions. Perhaps you will have developed new products or services. Perhaps you will find new customers or clients. Perhaps you will find new benefits that meet the wants of a substantial group of people.

Just be sure that the changes in these definitions provide very significant new opportunities that far overshadow what you have been doing. Frittering away your efforts on too many "opportunities" is a sure path to failure. Focus leads to success.

So What?

These three definitions are a very important beginning to the thinking tasks a leader must do. Other thinking tasks will follow, built on these definitions.

But before we get to these, I need to ask "So what?" You have the definitions but where will they take your organization? Any organization can only be successful if customers or clients actually purchase products or services. It is the money flowing from the purchases that makes it possible to sustain and grow the organization.

There are three key factors: customer or client *awareness*, customer or client *ability to pay*, customer or client *access*.

How do the customers or clients know about your product or service? If you haven't informed them about what you offer how can you expect them to make a purchase? Knowledge of your product or service must be conveyed to potential customers. Sometimes, this is difficult or impossible. If they don't know about your product or service, nothing will happen. Are there affordable and effective ways of creating *awareness*?

Can the customers or clients you have identified afford to purchase what your organization offers? Even if they know about your product or service, even if they want it, if they cannot afford to purchase it, nothing will happen. Do your customer or clients have the *ability to pay*?

Do your potential customers or clients have a convenient way to obtain your products or services? They may want it. They may be able to afford it. But if they have no reasonable way to obtain the product or service, nothing can happen.

Sometimes, potential customers or clients are too far away. Sometimes getting to where you provide the product or service is too difficult or too time-consuming. Sellers who use the Internet must have customers who have devices and access to the Internet.

If your product must be physically delivered, can this be done conveniently and economically for your customers? If clients must come to your site for service, can they do so conveniently and economically?

Do your customers or clients have *access*?

Perhaps you need to reconsider your definitions to be sure that potential customers or clients can be economically informed about your product or service, that they can afford to purchase it (or a third party can be convinced to pay for it), and that they can conveniently complete a purchase.

If you are uncertain about any of these items, you have work to do.

Informing customers or clients about your product or service is a major aspect of marketing. There are a great many books, articles, courses, and other ways to learn more about marketing. This book is not a marketing text.

But figuring out the most effective and economically feasible ways of informing customers or clients about your product or service is a critical task for any organization.

As a book publisher, bookstores were a primary channel for distributing my product. But if a book is placed on a back shelf of a large store, spine out, among thousands of other titles − with the hope that a customer will wander in, find that shelf, pull the book out, peruse it, and then be energized to take out the wallet and buy the book, that is a very unsatisfactory way to sell a book.

So just getting a book on the shelves of a bookstore was not likely to be very productive. We had to find a way to inform potential customers that the book existed and give them reasons to want to go to their local bookstore and ask for the title by name.

The same situation exists when a book is one among the millions listed by Amazon or Barnes & Noble on their web sites. A way must be found to get potential customers to search for the specific book in order for there to be a reasonable chance of a sale.

Of course, it would be nice to have commercials on the hot TV shows to promote the book. But TV commercials (like much other mass market advertising) are not affordable for most books. Other means had to be found to inform potential customers. That is likely to be the case with the product or service you offer.

Most marketing experts agree that word-of-mouth is the most powerful sales tool. "I just read this great book, you ought to read it..."

"We just had a great meal at the new restaurant downtown. You ought to try it..."

"The counselor at the center on First Street has really helped me. You ought to think about making a visit..."

And so on. Such recommendations from friends are the most powerful sales motivators. The task for an organization is to find ways to get favorable word-of mouth recommendations going.

Almost all of the pre-publication promotion work that book publishers do is aimed at getting those first movers to buy the book. If those first customers like the book, then the word-of-mouth will get started.

When the first edition of the first Harry Potter book came out, the publisher only printed 10,000 copies. No one could predict what the word-of-mouth would be. No one could predict how large the potential audience might be. So the publisher was very cautious.

For the last Harry Potter book, the first printing was 8,500,000 copies. Word-of-mouth was already very active as readers breathlessly awaited the last book. The audience had been identified. The publisher could print a huge number of copies with confidence.

Every organization needs to find ways to create a buzz among potential customers or clients that will lead to success. Perhaps one of Apple's greatest assets is the core of fans who eagerly await the company's new products and then are very active in spreading their enthusiasm to their friends, face-to-face or over various social media.

How can your organization build that kind of unpaid but vital support for your product or service?

Consider your first definition again. Do you have the kind of product or service that can generate vocal "fans"?

Have you clearly identified your potential customers or clients so that you can find and use the most effective and economical means of informing them and then getting them to be your enthusiastic and unpaid "sales force"?

Does your product or service effectively target the actual wants of the customers or clients? Do you provide them with real value, value that will turn them into effective supporters?

Having good definitions is very important. In many ways this chapter is the most important in the book. But good definitions don't mean anything if they aren't turned into purchases of your product or service, purchases that bring in the money that will grow and sustain your organization.

Keep in mind the three factors: awareness, ability to pay, and access. For potential customers or clients to become actual customers or clients, they must be aware of what you offer. They must be able to pay for it. And they must have access.

So when I asked "So what?" I hope you answered with a clear picture in your mind of how your organization turns the definitions you have outlined into sales that will make your organization financially successful.

Define Your Core Competencies:

Every successful organization has core competencies – capabilities that have made it successful and which set it apart from other organizations.

What does your organization do better than anyone else? What are its unique strengths? What differentiates your organization from its competitors (actual and potential?)

A critical core competency might be superior product design, or more effective service, or simpler and easier transactions, or higher quality, or other factors that provide your customers or clients with significant benefits that competitors cannot easily imitate.

It is very worthwhile to spend time identifying the core competencies of your organization. To do so may require some investigation for too often we don't really know what it is that customers or clients really value about our organization. And if the organization does something really well, but customers or clients don't care, then that is not a real core competency. A core competency must be something your organization does that attracts and holds customers or clients.

How do you find out what your organization does that grabs customers or clients? Ask. You should be talking to your customers or clients regularly. Ask them to tell you what it is about your organization they value. Why are they customers or clients of yours? If they don't identify core competencies that they value, your organization has a serious problem.

Leaders are often surprised when they ask. What the customers or clients value the most may be something no one in the organization had identified as a core competency. With this new information, the organization can focus more effort on using this previously unrecognized core competency to increase its success.

When core competencies have been identified, then you can consider how to build on them to grow your organization and make it more successful. Solid core competencies are the foundation for growth.

When you have identified the organization's core competencies you will have provided a valuable focus for future planning.

Sometimes, an organization can't really identify any core competencies that set it apart. Such an organization is unlikely to have a long and successful future. Competitors with real core competencies will push that organization aside. Lack of core competencies is a major barrier to success.

Defining your core competencies is yet another valuable definition, related to those you have addressed

There is one more definition you need to make.

Define what you and other principals want.

Why are you doing what you are doing? Why do you work hard for long hours? Is it for personal gain – money, status, power? Or do you have other motives?

You are the leader of an <u>organization</u>. The organization's success is what defines your success as a leader.

Money, status, and power are all by-products of the success of the organization. You can't have any of those things unless the organization is successful.

Outstanding leaders always put the organization first. Its success is uppermost. Personal success comes from the organization's success.

First, an organization must satisfy its customers or clients or it will not survive for long. But eventually the organization must also provide satisfactions to its principals. Their satisfactions, however they define them, will come from the organization's success.

If you have a board or other key leaders, be sure that they understand that unless the organization is successful they cannot be successful.

It is particularly important to be honest with yourself. What are your motivations?

I hope your primary motivation is to make your organization a success.

Many small and large organizations fail because the leader has focused solely on what he or she could get *out* of the organization. What you put *into* the organization is what will make it a success – and make you a success.

The most successful organizations have leaders who are focused on the success of the organization, not on their personal success. From the organization's success will come their personal success. Money, status, power flow to leaders when the organization they lead is successful.

It has been said many times: do what you love! Of course, if doing what you love cannot put food on the table, that is a problem. But in my experience, people who are passionate about what they are doing almost always end up having a reasonable income. (And often, those making scads of money hate what they are doing.)

Passion is a critical part of organizational success. If you and your other principals do not have a passion for what your organization is doing, your organization cannot hope to be the best in its field. From passion for the organization's success, comes personal success.

Defining what you want is not easy. It asks you to look deep within yourself and come up with an honest assessment of your own wants, your own requirements for personal satisfaction, your own commitment to the organization.

Let me repeat: you are the leader of an organization. The organization comes first. You can only be a successful leader when you have a successful organization.

Spend time on this definition. Talk with your spouse or partner or others who are close to you. Let them help you gain a clearer understanding of your own passion. I want you to be absolutely sure you have the passion for the organization that will lead you to make the commitment needed for its success – and thus your success.

* * * * *

Thinking through these definitions is hard work. To provide valuable guidelines for your organization's future you need to spend the time and effort. I promised you this book would not be a quick and easy read.

Should you do this by yourself? No. The definitions will be much sharper and much more useful if other people are involved.

If you are a small operation and don't have a team to work with, you may want to present the definitions you come up with to others, those working with you, and perhaps your spouse or your best friend. These other minds, other viewpoints can be very helpful.

They might say, "I understand what you are saying. It makes sense to me." Or they might say, "It sounds fuzzy. I can't really get a grip on what you mean." This kind of feed-back will be very helpful.

Be sure to involve the employees in your organization in creating the first three definitions. They will often bring different and important experiences and ideas to bear on these definitions.

In one business, a young man packing orders in the warehouse provided important input. He saw every day exactly which customers were ordering what products. He had developed a very good feel for who the customers were and what they wanted. Once he realized that his input would be valued, he opened up. Even though his boss had computer reports that provided much information, this young man made a significant contribution to good definitions.

In a social service agency, a young woman was on the front line. She was doing client intake, entering into the computer the client's name, age, address, and other information. But when the clients told her the basic data they often told her much more. They might explain the problem that brought them to the agency. They might explain why they chose that specific agency. They might tell about other agencies they had tried. This young woman at the intake desk had access to an enormous amount of valuable anecdotal information that the reports her superiors were getting could not convey. She was able to make a very valuable contribution to the definitions this agency prepared.

You will greatly improve your definitions if you bring in others to help. And when you ask employees to help you, you will be building greater trust and commitment.

Some organizations, even smaller ones, have more than one operation. I work with a small not-for-profit that has two divisions. Each division provides a very different service, and serves a very different client base. In this organization, the overall leader has tasked the leaders of each of the divisions to come up with definitions for their division.

Have you written down your definitions? Do they represent your best thinking?

The definitions now lead to the next chapter.

B. <u>THE MISSION</u>

When you have finished the definitions it is time to create a <u>mission statement</u>. This will become a public document that you can give to customers, clients, employees, bankers, donors, community leaders, and so on. It should be a short paragraph. Long, wordy mission statements are usually ignored or considered mostly hot air.

Perhaps you already have a mission statement. Many organizations do. But it is worthwhile to take another look at it.

The mission statement should tell *what* products or services you provide. This will come from your definition.

The mission statement should tell to *whom* you provide the products or services. This will come from your definition.

The mission statement also should briefly tell what is unique, special, or distinctive about either your product or service or the customers or clients you aim at. It is *how* you do what you do.

A well-thought-out mission statement, based on the work you have done on the definitions above, will keep you and everyone else associated with your business focused.

A good mission statement attracts. When potential customers or clients read it, they are attracted to your organization. When lenders or funders read it, they are more willing to deal with your organization. When potential employees, board members, or community leaders read your mission statement it should attract them to your organization. Be sure your mission statement will be a magnet that attracts.

The mission statement has another function. Attention to the mission keeps you from taking on activities that seem interesting, even useful, but which do not fit your mission. Too often leaders get seduced by attractive opportunities outside their mission. Too often these turn out not to be opportunities, but are distractions. (Remember my venture into indoor tennis courts.)

When considering opportunities, read your mission statement to be sure the opportunity fits the mission. If not, pass the opportunity up. It will only detract from your mission.

Success comes from focus. A good mission statement provides the focus.

Successful organizations review their definitions and their mission statements at least once a year. The review may suggest that changes are needed to refocus the organization. Or the review may help the organization avoid distracting opportunities.

Does your organization have a mission statement? When was it last reviewed? Does it attract?

Here is a brief selection of the mission statements of both for-profit companies and not-for-profit organizations. Read each one and decide if the mission statement tells what they do, who they do it for, how they do it. Is it attractive?

Which mission statements will help everyone involved with the organization to maintain focus and direction?

Advanced Auto Parts, Inc.
It is the mission of Advanced Auto Parts to provide personal vehicle owners and enthusiasts with the vehicle related products and knowledge that fulfill their wants and needs at the right price. Our friendly, knowledgeable, and professional staff will help, inspire, educate and problem-solve for our customers.

Ameren
Ameren's mission is to generate electricity, deliver electricity and distribute natural gas in a safe, reliable, efficient and environmentally sound manner…we will achieve operational excellence, industry-leading customer satisfaction and superior financial performance.

ADM
ADM Mission: To unlock the potential of nature to improve the quality of life.

Bristol-Myers Squibb Company
To discover, develop and deliver innovative medicines that help patients prevail over serious diseases.

Family Dollar Store
For Our customers A compelling place to shop...by providing convenience and low prices. For Our Associates A compelling place to work...by providing exceptional opportunities and rewards for achievement. For Our Investors A compelling place to invest...by providing outstanding returns.

Ford
We are a global family with a proud heritage passionately committed to providing personal mobility for people around the world.

The Hershey Company
Undisputed Marketplace Leadership

Manpower
To be the best worldwide provider of high-value staffing services and the center for quality employment opportunities.

Springboard
Our mission is simple: To offer education on the wise use of credit.

Angels in Care
Our MISSION is to be a Refuge in which Children who are hurting Emotionally, Mentally or Physically can find Love, Hope, Peace & Joy.

The Saint Paul Foundation
Our mission is to actively serve the people of the East Metro area by building permanent charitable capital, making philanthropic

grants, and providing services that contribute to the health and vitality of the community.

Metropolitan Area Agency on Aging
In partnership with public and private organizations, MAAA helps elders age successfully. It does this by building community capacity, advocating for aging issues, maximizing service effectiveness and linking people with information.

Goodwill Industries of North Georgia
We put people to work.

I hope you have read these mission statements with a critical eye. Which are attractive, which are hot air?

You can find many more examples of mission statements on the Internet. Look for the ones that are magnets.

How would your mission statement be evaluated? Would an outsider find it attracting? Or would it be considered hot air?

If you don't have a mission statement, you need to create one, with the help of key employees, board members, and others. If you already have a mission statement, now is the time to review it.

C. __VALUES__

Our activities in life are guided by our values. You may not have consciously articulated what your values are, but they act to influence your behavior.

In the same way, your organization needs to have values that guide its activities. The values need to support the mission. Your mission statement will be so much hot air if it is not based upon values that are in harmony with the mission.

What are the key values that you want to be ingrained in your organization, values that will guide everyday actions to achieve the mission?

Perhaps you already know what values you want to guide your organization. Are they written down? If they have been written down are they are in visible places where you can refer to them frequently, especially as difficult issues arise.

You need to take steps to identify the values that are critical for your organization. Then you need to take steps to have these values guide your organization's activities.

If the staff doesn't know the values or doesn't buy into the values, the values won't have much impact on the day-to-day operations. You need to involve your staff in identifying the critical values that the organization will live by. Perhaps you have a set of written-down values that are well-known to the staff. If not, here are some ideas.

I suggest that you write down the values you believe the organization should hold to. Then put that document in the desk drawer.

Assemble your staff – all at once for a small staff, perhaps in several sessions for a large staff. Tell them in advance that the meeting will focus on identifying values that you and the staff will want to live by as the organization operates.

Ask for suggestions for values. These should be brief sentences. Have a staff member write the sentences proposed by members of the group on an easel, blackboard, whiteboard, or some other surface where all can read the sentences. Ask each member of the group to propose one or more value statements they believe are important to organizational success.

You do not say anything at this step in the process, except to encourage input and see that the sentences clearly state the value that is proposed.

When the group seems have proposed all the value statements they are likely to have you can then ask the group to choose the top four, five, or six values they believe are critical to the organization's success and that should guide what they do every day.

This is a time for you to gently suggest any values you believe are vital that the staff has not come up with.

"I wonder if this is a value we ought to consider…..?" Use questions rather than direct statements. Remember, you want the staff to buy into the values. This is more likely to happen if the values don't seem to be handed down from the leader, but come from the staff who have to live by them when you are not around to remind everybody.

Once the value statements have been agreed upon, you need to get them put into useful formats. I have printed cards to give to each employee, old or new. As with the mission statement, I printed a poster to put up on the bulletin board, in the break room, or wherever else it would be a regular reminder.

The values won't mean much if you, the leader, don't live by them. If your staff sees you cutting corners, ignoring a value you said was important, you will not be able to expect the staff to pay any attention to the values.

Perhaps you will fail to live up to a value in some situation. Then admit it openly and acknowledge that you will work to see that you live by the values as you expect others to do.

The purpose of articulating the organization's values is to help each member of your staff to know how to act in an ambiguous situation where you or the supervisors are not around to tell staff what to do.

41

In most organizations, employees face many situations where they must decide what to do on their own. You want them to do what will provide the greatest long-term benefit to the organization.

Enunciating primary values and seeing that employees know them well will help take care of this.

There are lots of questions that arise, in dealing with customers or clients, in dealing with suppliers, in dealing with others. These often come up without warning, where action or answers are immediately required. You can't be everywhere to see that those questions are handled properly.

But your organizational values can be everywhere in the organization, to be the guideposts for right actions.

So spend time and effort to work through the process to establish the values you want your staff to act on.

Some years ago, a set of values was developed for an organization I led. We talked about the values with the staff. We gave each staff member a card with the values enunciated in brief sentences. We frequently celebrated employees who made special contributions to upholding one or another value. We tried to keep the values always in our minds.

The values described below are the values we developed.

The customer comes first!

That was the first and most important value for me. Our success was totally dependent upon the customers. When an employee faced a decision, one that perhaps would cost the company money, they could always ask themselves, "What will be best for the customer?" They would know there would be no criticism from their supervisor if they put the customer first. (Of course, within limits.)

A lot of organizations say they put the customer first. But they don't. An organization that serves families where both spouses usually work opens at 9:00 AM, closes for an hour at lunch, and shuts down at 5:00 PM. Are they putting their customers or clients first? Or is the convenience of the staff more important?

Such an organization needs to find a way to restructure its hours to accommodate the two-earner families they hope to serve.

It is all too easy to make employee convenience more important than customer service.

You can surely think of other examples where organizations do not put the customer first.

Employees are the key to success!

This says the organization values its employees and recognizes that it is their efforts that will make the organization successful.

Lots of organizations say they value employees, but their actions say otherwise.

When times are tough, does the organization make a mass lay-off or does it do everything possible to keep its employees, even if only on part-time?

No leader can be everywhere, doing everything. Good employees – the right people – make all the difference to an organization.

Our company provided software for the critical operations of customers, often far away from our location. One such customer had tried to add some functions to the software by using their own in-house people to do the coding. The system crashed.

The customer called our local representative for help. Of course, it was the customer that caused the problem. But quickly the local representative enlisted a software engineer from the company. Both arrived at the customer's location. After some complicated work, the problem was fixed, the software was up and running – and the function the customer had tried to insert was put into the system. All this was done at significant cost to the company and no charge to the customer.

These employees knew what to do and did it. There was never any question about how to respond. The customer comes first! And the employees went out of their way and created a very satisfied customer who could and did talk about how great the company was to come to the rescue. Employees are the key to success!

Always do the right thing, the ethical thing!

I strongly believe that bad actions produce bad results. Most employees want to work in an organization that lives up to their ethical expectations. They need to know that this is a key value that the leader supports absolutely (and expects them to support.)

Sometimes doing the right thing costs money, where cutting ethical corners might produce a better immediate result. Employees need to know that the leader will support them when they make the ethical decision.

I was trying to sell to a major potential customer in another state. After meeting with the person who would make the decision, I went back to my hotel. In the lobby, a well-dressed man came up to me.

"Your products are the best. The buyer is ready to select them tomorrow. But the selection would surely happen if you could see your way to making some funds available to the buyer for personal expenses. Of course, you don't have to, but a small investment would clinch the deal."

In other words, a bribe would get us the business.

Our ethical standards were in conflict with the opportunity to obtain a really big order. What should I do?

I thought of the value, "Always do the right thing, the ethical thing." I didn't pay the bribe. I didn't get the business. That was painful, but it seemed to have beneficial long-term consequences. Other potential customers recognized us as the kind of ethical company they wanted to deal with. Employees saw this value in action. I like to think that in the end, more business came our way than we lost.

Ethical behavior was such an important value that we developed an "Ethics Pledge." This contained a general statement of the company's position on ethical behavior and then specific statements regarding such matters as bribes, cheating, lying, and so on. This Pledge was given to all new employees and they were asked to read it and sign it.

Did this completely eliminate unethical actions? Probably not, but it certainly made employees much more aware of the ethical standards they were expected to meet. Reading and signing the Pledge was an action that made it much more difficult to behave unethically.

Innovation is necessary!

I never wanted my staff to think we could stand pat, that our products and procedures were so good they would not ever need improvement. I encouraged everyone to come up with ideas for improvement, even ideas for entirely new products or customer groups.

The staff understood many ideas might not be practical or timely. But they also understood that one really good innovation might take the organization, and them, to entirely new heights of success. ("We've always done it this way…" was not an acceptable stance if this value was to be honored.)

Profits are essential!

In my for-profit organization, I never wanted any employee to forget that we had to be profitable. A profitable organization would ensure their jobs and make it possible to give them raises. Profits were the basis for the investments needed in new products, new processes, new opportunities. No profits and the organization would cease to exist, along with its jobs.

In not-for-profit organizations, it isn't called "profit." But the organization better take in more money than it pays out. It needs a surplus with which to take on new opportunities or counter problems. Employees in these organizations also need to understand that their jobs depend upon the organization's ability to create a surplus (or "profit.")

So these are the values I worked very hard to communicate and to make the bed-rock foundation for the organization.

What are the values you, as a leader, want your organization to live by? Go through the process to establish your organization's critical values. Then articulate them, put them into many written documents to remind staff, and make the values part of every decision.

D. <u>THE VISION FOR THE FUTURE</u>

If you don't know where you want to go, you probably won't get there. So, the next thinking activity is to create a <u>vision</u> for the organization. This involves conceptualizing, then writing down what you want the organization to become in five years. What are your goals for the organization five years from now?

Of course, you want the organization to be a success five years from now. But what does that mean?

One consultant offered this suggestion. Imagine that you are kidnapped and are held for five years with no communication with the outside world. Now you are released and restored to your organization. What will you find when you come back after five years away? What will the organization be doing? What will it look like?

Certainly this is one way to approach the creation of a vision. You want to describe your organization as you hope to see it five years from now. What products or services will it be offering? Who will its customers be? Will the customers have different wants? What challenges will affect the organization five years from now?

The vision needs to be concrete and specific about all of the aspects of the organization five years from now.

This should be a fun thinking exercise. It lets you dream about all that could be. Of course, the dream needs to be based on realistic probabilities.

I have found that creating a vision is difficult for some people. One leader told me, "This vision business is a waste of time. I just want to keep on growing at a nice comfortable pace."

"What would that be?" I asked.

"Well, six or seven percent growth a year would be about right." He replied.

I had to smile. "You know," I told him, "seven percent a year will make your organization forty percent larger in five years. Will you be able to be that much larger with the same products you are providing, the same customers, the same number of employees?"

Here is a hypothetical conversation with the leader of Acme Widgets, the mythical company whose planning you will encounter later in this book.

Me: Where do you want Acme to be in five years?

Acme Leader: We should be the dominant company in our market.

Me: What does that mean? How many widgets will you be selling five years from now? Will they be the same kind of widgets you are selling now? Or will you have expanded the product line and upgraded your current products?

Acme Leader: Of course, we will have to upgrade and to add new widget products.

Me: How many of each kind, at what prices, do you expect to be selling in five years? You need to think this through because that leads to the question of what kinds of machines you will need to produce these widgets. And then, what staffing and what facilities will you need to produce, sell, and distribute all those widgets that will make you the dominant company in five years?

Acme Leader: It sounds like I better be a lot more specific about what Acme Widgets will look like in five years. The vision needs to be concrete, doesn't it?

My advice would be to start off with envisioning what your organization will look like in five years – its revenues, the number and mix of customer or clients, the products or services, and so on. Put down on paper a snapshot of your organization five years from now, as you want it to be. Be specific and be detailed.

Look back at your definitions and think about how each one will have developed over the next five years.

What are likely to be the products or services that the organization will be providing? Will you expand your offerings or will you be offering the same products and services in five years? How might your products or services change over the years? Are there likely to be external factors that will make your products or services obsolete in five years? If so, how will you reshape your organization's offerings to stay in business?

Who will be the customers or clients in five years? Will your organization be serving the same group of customers or clients? Will the numbers and/or geographical spread of your customers or clients have increased? Or do you expect to be serving the same customers or clients that you serve now? Perhaps the future will bring such changes that you will need to target an entirely different set of customers or clients.

What are the benefits and values that your customers or clients are likely to want in the future? Will there be circumstances that will require your organization to change or refine your products or services so that they meet the evolving wants of the customers or clients? Could you make major changes?

What kinds of satisfactions will the organization be providing to its principals in five years? Will you and other principals in the organization still maintain commitment and dedication in five years? Will the job still be fun and challenging? Can you expect adequate financial rewards? What other kinds of rewards from the organization should be planned for over the coming five years?

Finally, you need to clearly think through the potential dangers that may arise over the five-year period. There is no doubt that technology will change and evolve. How will the likely developments in technology affect your organization?

Governments will take various actions. These could include new regulations, changes in the tax laws, and even competition from government agencies.

It is now necessary to ask what organizations in other countries might do that would seriously impact your operations. Of course, there will be competition closer at hand. (These and other barriers to success are discussed in the next chapter.)

Think about the external factors that could have a dramatic impact upon your activities over the five-year span of your vision. A vision that guides action must carefully address all of the facets we have been discussing here.

Creating the five-year vision, like the other thinking tasks, requires much thought. But, without a clear vision, you will certainly not get where you want to be in the future.

The vision sometimes seems like an "airy-fairy" exercise, not worth the time and effort. Action now is what is important. But without a clear vision you may end up going around in circles. There will be a lot of action but no progress. Defining where you want the organization to be five years from now will give you a goal to pursue.

You can see that the definitions lead to the mission statement. The definitions and the mission statement lead to the vision. Perhaps you have defined your product or service so narrowly that there is no room for growth. The same may be true of the customers or clients you have defined. On the other hand, definitions that are too broad do not provide sharp enough focus.

Especially for new or small businesses, a sharp focus is essential. You don't have the resources – time, money, energy, staff – to take on a broad line of products or services. Nor can you go after too wide an audience. Your vision can be for a broader offering and a wider customer/client base in five years. It should be. But you can't grow a new or small operation and get it off the ground if you are not sharply focused.

For established operations, a good vision will build upon the strengths you have already established.

My friend Nora runs a small manufacturing business. She has been working through the various thinking tasks and has helped me to sharpen this book.

She thought about the vision for her company – where she wanted it to be in five years.

Her first thought was, "Will I be here in five years?" She decided that she did indeed intend to be leading the company five years in the future. Of course, other leaders may look to retirement or to other life changes that would mean they would not be at the head of their organization in five years. (Then who would be?)

Nora planned to stay on, but she wanted the company to be a different one in five years.

Her company makes parts that are sold to two large manufacturers. She knew she wanted a broader customer base so her company could survive if one customer went away. She had done the selling to the two current customers. But to get more customers, the company would likely need someone on board to call on and sell to a broader base.

Of course, Nora wanted the company to grow. She thought about what the company might look like in five years. There would be a larger, more diversified customer group. The products her company made and sold would grow as well. She conceptualized several possible product areas that could build on the company's core competencies.

That led to consideration of what kind of facilities the company would need in five years and what kind of staff would be needed. There would be additional machines. She thought of what she knew about evolving technologies and how they might affect the kinds of machines, and indeed, all of the operations of the business in five years.

She put all of these thoughts – her vision for the company – down on paper.

Then she gathered her key staff and asked them to come up with their vision for the company. The staff members were given a week to think about this, then they all got together with Nora for a half-day session.

She organized things into areas. First, the group talked about sales revenues. How many dollars would be coming in the door in five years? And then, where would those dollars come from? What products? What customers?

The group went through the various areas that Nora had already thought about (and raised some she had not thought about.) Nora's own work on envisioning the company in five years helped her to keep the meeting moving forward. From time to time, she had to gently step in to bring up a point the others had missed.

When the session was over, Nora asked her next-in-command to write up the conclusions that would form the vision. This vision was the lead-in to other important thinking tasks.

I looked on the Internet for vision statements as I had done for mission statements. All the public vision statements I found read like mission statements. They did not define where the organization hoped to be in five years. And they were too short to really be useful.

And of course, most organizations do not want to publish their real vision. It might help competitors. You probably won't want to make your vision public, as you have with the mission statement.

But it needs to become known to the key people in the organization. They need to know (and perhaps help in thinking through) where the organization is headed, where it hopes to be in five years. If they buy into the vision, they will be more focused on how what they do today can lead toward the desirable status of the organization in five years. Everyone wants to know that the future holds good things for them.

Of course, the vision cannot be just rosy hopes for a bright future. It needs to be based on a realistic assessment of what is possible.

When you have created this detailed vision of the future, you need to build a road map of how to get there.

E. <u>THE BARRIERS TO SUCCESS</u>

Before we get to the road map to reach the vision that outlines what you hope and expect your organization and its business will be like in five years you need to think about what <u>barriers</u> may arise that will prevent the vision from being achieved.

Some years ago, Bill Gates wrote what became known as the "nightmare memo." It outlined all of the problems that might arise to derail Microsoft's success. At the time the company was quite successful. It looked to become even more successful. But Gates wanted to remind himself and his staff of the possible barriers that Microsoft might face. By writing these down he and his staff could think about how to prepare for events that might never occur, but which, if they did, would create great difficulties for the company.

A good leader thinks about potential problems so as not to be blind-sided.

What are the possible difficulties that could derail your organization? Let me suggest some categories.

Competition: What competitors are out there who might undermine your operations? Think about existing competitors. But also think about what organizations might decide to enter your field of activity, perhaps with new approaches, new technology, or better service. In the global economy, there could be competitors in distant countries as well as next door. You already know about existing competition. Presumably, you have taken steps to deal with this. But you need to think about what competitors could arise in the future, ones that might threaten your organization. What can you do to become and remain the top organization in your field or your area, in the face of unexpected competition?

It is worthwhile to write down your thoughts about possible future competition.

Nora's company had a few U.S. competitors, but a Chinese company had already called upon her customers. She would need to carefully consider how to deal with competition from Asian companies with low labor costs.

She decided that her location, much closer to the customers, was an advantage. She and her staff researched new digitally-controlled laser machines that could greatly increase production with far lower labor costs. Of course, financing the purchase of these machines had to be thought through. But she could see ways to outcompete Asian competitors.

Governments: What might local, state, or national governments do that would seriously impact your organization? Are there new taxes likely in the five years of your vision? Could there be new regulations that hamper your operations? Do you depend on government protection of intellectual property such as patents or copyrights? Could that protection weaken? If government funding is important to your organization, could this be reduced or eliminated in future years? How could your organization survive and prosper in the face of negative government actions?

Put down on paper the government actions that could affect your organization in the future.

Nora sat down with her accountant to talk about what was likely to happen with taxes. His firm received much information from Washington and the state capital that helped to predict the future course of taxes.

Suppliers: Do you depend on just a few key suppliers? What if one of them went broke or decided to no longer do business with you? How could you operate in such a situation? What alternatives could be developed? Should you start looking now?

Nora knew she needed to broaden her base of suppliers and her purchasing manager was tasked with this job.

Employees: Do you have key employees whose departure would seriously impact the organization? What can you do to be prepared for such an eventuality? (Cross-training is an important activity to prepare for the possible departure of a key employee.)

Are any of your employees in a union? If not, could they be attracted by union organizers? What might unionization of your employees mean to the organization?

Nora had people she considered key employees. Their departure would cause a serious problem, at least until replacements could be found and trained. But in her small company, there was no possibility of adding staff who might be back-ups. She reviewed the pay of these key employees. She talked with them, especially about how important they were to achieving the five-year vision that they had all arrived at.

Funders: Does your organization depend upon outside funders, such as banks or other lenders? What if a lender decides to end your relationship? What if your line of credit is cut? Where could you find other sources of funds to maintain your operations?

If you are a nonprofit, you may depend upon foundation or government grants. What if these dry up?

Perhaps you will want to begin investigating other sources of funding should you need them in the future.

Too Rapid Growth: This may seem like an odd one. You want to grow. How could growth be too fast? If you are beyond the start-up stage, too rapid growth can cause serious problems in customer service, delivery, cash flow, and other areas. It can burn out employees, even cause them to leave.

Too rapid growth can leave your organization overextended in many ways and make the organization vulnerable to failure. Mature organizations need to resist growing too rapidly. They need to grow at a sustainable pace. That takes discipline, the ability to say "no" to promising high-growth opportunities that will over-stretch the organization.

A major issue with too rapid growth is cash. It almost always takes up-front cash to fund growth. The cash flow from the growth usually comes in after the organization has had to invest cash. Too rapid growth may over-stretch cash resources, put the organization in a precarious position, and even lead to failure.

Could you get in a situation where your growth was too fast for your resources?

Nora thought that the growth projected to reach the five-year vision was ambitious but doable. Cash would be needed. She sat down with her banker and showed her the five-year vision. They discussed what this would mean in terms of loan requirements for the company. Nora wanted to be sure that her banker understood where the company was going and be sure that the bank would be prepared to make funds available to supplement the funds that company profits would provide.

**Natural Disasters**: It seems that more and more natural disasters are occurring – tornados, hurricanes, floods, earthquakes, blizzards, power outages, and many more. Any one of these could bring your organization's activities to a sudden halt. And worse, destroy your computer files or records, ruin your stock of goods, or even completely smash your facilities. What would you and your organization do if such a disaster occurred?

You need to think about these worst- case scenarios and make plans for how to deal with them. Be sure your insurance provides sufficient coverage so that a big storm doesn't leave you with no way to recover.

All your critical records should have back-up files that are stored somewhere else with less likelihood of loss or damage.

How will you notify customers or clients, suppliers, and especially staff, when a natural disaster shuts your operations down?

These are just a few of the considerations that a natural disaster would require you to deal with.

There needs to be a written disaster plan that outlines key steps to be taken as well as the location of back-up information and the contact information for key personnel who could be at home or elsewhere when disaster strikes.

You and your key personnel each need a copy of the disaster plan to keep at home. You might be away on a trip when a disaster struck and others would have to step in to handle the situation. Be sure they are prepared.

(The Internet has information on creating a good disaster plan.)

We all hope none of these disasters ever occur to us. But it is foolhardy to imagine that your organization will never face such a problem. Be prepared!

Technology: We can be certain that technology will change. New technologies we cannot imagine will impact the organization. Only a few years ago, few could have imagined the impact of the Internet. But many organizations that ignored this development are now gone, replaced by organizations that grabbed hold of this new technology.

There will certainly be equally earth-shaking technologies coming in the future. You need to do your best to keep abreast of new developments that could significantly impact your organization. Reading, attending conferences, talking with other people who are working in fields that might affect you are ways to try to anticipate and prepare for new technological advances that could either obsolete your organization or give it entirely new opportunities.

Of course, many of the hot technologies being breathlessly discussed won't occur or will have minimal impact on your organization. You need to be discriminating as you consider the potential technologies being developed.

But it is clear that new technologies will affect your organization. Some could be significant barriers to your success as others might lead you to even great success.

Others: What other nightmares are lurking out there to cause serious problems for your organization? It is far better to think about them before they actually happen. Probably, most of the nightmares you conjure up will not occur. But if one or another does, you will be far better prepared to deal with it for having done this thinking task.

Take time to write up the possible problems that might occur and set down plans for how to deal with them. Then, should a nightmare come to life, your organization will be able to deal with it

There will always be unpleasant surprises. But good organizations can adjust and cope. Poor organizations often fail because they haven't considered how to deal with unexpected surprises.

Succession: There is one last item that needs to be considered. What if you were hit by the proverbial streetcar tomorrow? Do you have plans for succession? Is someone being trained to step into your shoes? Is there someone to take your place if you might not be around sometime in the future?

In small organizations these are difficult questions, often with no definitive answers. But it is a valuable exercise to consider how the organization would move forward in your absence or in the absence of other key employees. If you put the organization's survival and success at the top of your priorities, then it is necessary to think about what really ought to be the unthinkable.

In a small organization it often seems that everyone is indispensable. But no one is. And everyone is susceptible to an unexpected event that would remove them from the organization. Think about this. Especially, think about what should happen if you were incapacitated.

As a leader responsible for an organization, planning for succession is an important responsibility.

There are many potential barriers to your organization's success. Let's hope none of them occur. But the time spent preparing to deal with barriers will keep your organization alive should any of them occur.

F. <u>THE STRATEGIC PLAN</u>

When the vision is defined and the possible barriers identified, it is time to create a <u>strategic plan</u>. The plan outlines how the organization will get from its present state to where you want it to be in five years.

The leader of Acme Widgets can now put numbers to his vision. What dollar revenues will come from the sales of the widgets he envisions in five years? He will need to think through other financial aspects of his vision.

Nora's group had already set down the revenues they expected in five years, as well as other numbers related to their vision of the future. Now they needed to create a five-year plan that would take the company from its current situation to the place they wanted it to be in five years. Each of the five years would need to be planned.

A strategic plan in essence creates a budget for each of the five years leading to the vision you have created. A good strategic plan involves several considerations. I believe you should start with cash flow.

1. <u>Cash Flow</u>:

You can't stay in business and achieve the five-year vision without cash. Cash is absolutely essential to survival and success.

What cash flow, in and out, will be needed to accomplish the vision? Often budgets are put together in accounting terms. But accounting is a system of keeping score in business. It does not tell actual flows of cash. A successful organization over time must have more cash coming in than is going out.

A cash flow budget plans on where the cash will come from and when it will come. It plans on when the cash going out will have to be paid.

In many businesses, customers pay slowly, often months after their purchase (or perhaps not at all.) Nonprofits often receive grants or contract payments many months after the organization has had to pay salaries, rent, and so on.

Organizations usually have to pay out cash before cash comes in. An expanding organization may need more space in which to operate. Growth may require more furniture and equipment and often additional machinery. All these things must be paid for, with cash.

A business growing toward its five-year vision will probably need to add staff. Their salaries and payroll taxes have to be paid, often before they produce income. Where will the cash come from for these expenditures?

Of course, the owners of a business have usually made an investment. Profits (or surplus) generated from operations provide cash. Then banks or other lenders may provide some of the needed cash. Nonprofits may seek grants or donations to get the cash needed to grow.

To achieve the vision you have, cash flow is necessary. You need to be sure that the cash flow is sufficient.

Preparing a cash flow budget makes you think through the requirements for cash. And of course, if the cash flow budget shows that cash coming in is never going to catch up with the cash paid out, then it is clear that a successful operation will not be possible.

I cannot stress enough the critical importance of preparing a long-term cash flow budget. Too many leaders do not do this. And often they find that their organization is unable to pay the bills. Their dreams and hopes are dashed on the hard reality of cash in vs. cash out.

(A recent survey found that small business owners named cash flow problems as their biggest concern.)

A warning for start-ups: However much cash you think you need, however much time you think is necessary, it takes more cash and more time than you think it will to provide an organization with the basis for long-term success. My experience has always been that more cash and more time were needed than I originally planned for.

It takes a lot of hard thinking to do a good cash flow budget over the five years of the strategic plan. It is thinking time and effort that will be repaid many times over. And if you go to investors or bankers or major donors, a good cash flow plan will be essential to convincing them to provide you with funds.

In the Appendix, you will find a three-year cash flow budget for Acme Widgets, a mythical company created to provide you with a concrete example. If you are not familiar with cash flow planning spend some time studying this. It will give you a better understanding of how to prepare this essential plan. The Acme Widget cash flow budgets show some of the primary categories of cash in and cash out that need to be in the plan.

In larger organizations, it may be the financial/accounting people who put the numbers down for the cash flow budget. But the basis for those numbers must come from the thinking and planning the leader has done (often with the team.)

One more thought: as you work on a five-year cash flow plan, you may find that it leads to rethinking the previous work you have done. Perhaps your five-year vision is too expansive. It cannot be financed. You need to rethink it and trim it, or else consider how it might be financed.

Perhaps you need to go as far back as the definitions to consider them again in light of the potential cash flow. If the maximum potential revenues you thought about when considering customers and clients are insufficient to bring in enough cash to support your plans, then something has to be changed.

You will likely find it necessary (and desirable) to reconsider your definitions and your vision as these meet the realities of cash flow.

Let me emphasize again that the usual accounting reports don't clearly show cash in and cash out. The financial reports that are prepared for tax purposes and that usually are given to boards and others do not provide the information you need to understand the flow of cash.

Nora and her key staff spent much time on planning the company's cash needs, year by year through the five years of the vision they had created. They met for a couple of hours each week to work on this. When they were finished, Nora took the plan to the bank so that her banker would understand what funds would be needed and when. With the plan that had been created and the involvement of the bank, Nora felt confident that the company could achieve the vision.

2. **Organization:**

Now you need to think through your organization and staffing. To reach your five-year vision, how must your organization be structured? What kind of people will you need to bring on board to make the vision a reality? What will those people do? When will you need them? How much will they cost?

As your operation grows in size and complexity, toward the five-year vision you have set, you will almost certainly need more people to handle the work.

Perhaps you already have good people working in your organization. You may already have a sizeable staff. But will they be sufficient to achieve the vision?

What kind of people will you need for the future? When will you need them? Where will you find them? This thinking task involves writing down job descriptions for the key positions you plan for.

It is a good idea to make up organization charts that shows the positions in your organization and their relation to one another. The organization will probably change over the period of your vision, so the charts need to reflect those changes. How will your organization have to be structured in five years?

Some organization charts are hierarchical. They look like a pyramid. Other charts use the matrix format. They are much more flat and not pyramid-shaped. Different kinds of organizations need different kinds of charts because they require different relationships.

Your organization chart should reflect the most effective and efficient way of organizing your staff.

We will have a later section on the preparation of useful job descriptions, ones that will help you find the right person and then be able to evaluate if that person is actually accomplishing the job you need done.

(Many other resources cover organizational structure in great detail. I won't try to cover this here.)

The organization plan, like the cash flow plan, needs to be for each of the five years of the strategic plan. How many new people, if any, will be needed in the first year of the plan? In the second year? And so on for all five years.

As you plan for the addition of staff, with their salaries and payroll taxes, these costs need to be incorporated into the five-year cash flow budget.

What other resources will be necessary to accomplish your vision? Will you need more space? When? Will you need more equipment? What kind? When? What other resources are going to be needed to get where you want to be in five years?

Prepare a written list of these. The list should show what you will need, when you will need it, and how much it is likely to cost. (The cost and the timing will need to be part of the cash flow budget.)

The five-year plan needs to include the financial and non-financial benefits the leader, owners, and directors of the organization will receive. And of course, the financial benefits need to be part of the cash flow budget, especially planned dividends or distributions. Often, these are not planned for and often they don't happen. And when owners expect dividends or distributions that don't occur, the organization cannot last.

Nora's company would need additional people to reach the vision that had been set out. She already had a company organization chart so she put in the positions that would be added, following up with brief job descriptions. This was done for each year of the plan.

She assigned the production manager to research the new machines that might give the company a competitive advantage.

Preparing a strategic plan over a five-year period is not an easy task. If you have a clear vision of where you want the organization to go, then preparing a strategic plan that gets the organization there will be easier.

It is common in five-year planning that the fourth and fifth years feel a little fuzzy. There are too many unknowns that far into the future. But there are many benefits that come from making a plan that goes out the full five years. Thinking about those later years, in relation to your vision, will get you thinking about many aspects of the organization and how what you do in the coming year will affect the subsequent years.

A great many organizations have not taken the time or made the effort to create a five-year strategic plan. They may feel it is unnecessary or too time-consuming. Such organizations too often get into trouble that could have been avoided by thinking and planning for the longer-term future.

Creating a five-year strategic plan is not a one-time exercise. The five-year strategic plan needs to be revised every year. When the organization has completed the first year of the plan you now need to reconsider the upcoming years and add a new fifth year. Before you update the five-year strategic plan, it pays to review the definitions, the mission, and the vision to be sure that events have not required these to change, thus necessitating the strategic plan to be altered. If you have done a good job of thinking through these items, they probably will need little or no change. But don't assume that.

Change is always going on. It is an unavoidable factor in our lives and in the life of any organization. You must recognize change and adapt to it to be successful. A sound plan can easily incorporate most changes. In the five years of your plan, there are likely to be unexpected events – good luck or bad luck. But if you have a well-thought-out plan it can be easily altered to reflect these events and accommodate to them.

A good strategic plan supports the mission, honors the values, and provides the road map to achieve the vision. It is a very important foundation for success. It is well worth spending the time and effort to prepare this very valuable guide to the future you want.

G. <u>THE ANNUAL BUDGET</u>

The thinking tasks are not yet done. You now need to take your strategic plan and create a specific plan for the immediate future. This means a <u>budget</u> for the coming year, a budget that will move the organization toward its long-range vision. The annual budget will be more detailed than the strategic plan. But the strategic plan was, in essence, a budget for each of the five years of the plan.

Now you can take the first year of the strategic plan and turn it into a budget for the coming year.

I assume you already prepare an annual budget. Most organizations do that. But now that you have gone through the previous thinking tasks you can prepare a much more sharply focused budget.

The budget would, of course, include a cash flow budget. Presumably, you already considered cash flow in and out for this period when the strategic plan was developed.

It is common for budgets to follow the accrual accounting format – the typical income statement. But this can lead to a budget that has a fine bottom line – net income – but which has a negative cash flow.

It is quite possible to have a cheery accounting profit while the organization is going broke. I have seen companies that reported significant profits when they couldn't rustle up enough cash to buy a cup of coffee, much less pay salaries or suppliers. So the budget should be a cash flow budget. And if cash out exceeds cash in, you must then plan on how to right this imbalance. We will talk about this later on.

I keep pushing for cash flow budgeting because cash control is essential to success. But most financial reports to shareholders, owners, lenders, and donors are in the accrual accounting format. Quite often, organizations are required to present budgets in the accrual accounting format rather than in the cash flow accounting format. The IRS requires reporting in the accrual accounting format for most organizations. You will see the numbers in this format far more often than in the cash flow format, even though cash flow is essential to plan and control.

Here is a very simplified explanation of the difference. The cash flow accounting format keeps track of when actual cash flows in and when cash flows out. The accrual accounting format records revenues and expenses when the obligation occurs, which is often not when cash flows.

When customers are billed (but have not yet paid), the accrual accounting report shows sales revenue, even though no cash has come in yet.

When the organization buys something that will be paid for later, the expense shows up when the commitment is made, not when the actual cash is paid out.

When a major purchase – a building, a machine, etc. – is made, cash goes out to pay for the purchase. But this cash expenditure gets charged against the organization's expenses over the life of the purchase on an accrual accounting report. This depreciation or amortization expense is spread out over the expected life of the purchase. That could be twenty years. The annual financial report might show a depreciation or amortization expense as only one-twentieth of the actual cash paid out. All of the cash was paid out for the purchase. Only part of the cash payment shows up as an expense for the year.

Because accrual accounting reports do not show actual cash flowing in and out, they can be very misleading about the actual cash position of the organization. But this report format has become the accounting standard. You will probably see the accrual accounting report often. But remember that it does not show the real cash situation.

(My book, *How to Keep Score in Business: Accounting and Financial Analysis for the Non-Accountant,* explains all this in detail.)

Your organization's annual budget needs to be a cash basis budget to keep everyone focused on that critical element.

Another part of the budgeting process is the staffing budget. When do you take on more staff? What are their job descriptions? Of course, the costs of the additional staff are included in the cash flow budget for the year.

When do you take on more space, get more equipment? How much will this cost and when will it need to be paid for? This too goes into the cash flow budget.

There are many parts to a good annual budget. It starts, of course, with revenues. Where will your revenues come from? What products or services will you sell during the year? To whom will you sell them to? When can you expect to be paid? The budgeted cash revenue stream should exceed the budgeted cash expenditures. If not, you know you will have to find other sources of cash. The cash flow budget for the year needs to show where the additional cash is going to come from to keep the organization in business.

An annual cash flow budget will be a critical part of planning for success.

"Oh, oh, oh!" you are saying. "My head hurts from all this thinking. I just want to get on with my business."

Too many people do just that. And soon they are mired in a mess. They don't know where they are going. They have no idea how to get wherever it is they are going. They run out of cash. *Doing* without *thinking, action* without *planning,* is a sure formula for failure.

If you are not spending time thinking about your business, using the planning template we have been discussing (or another similar one), you will surely get into trouble. Failure is almost guaranteed for those unwilling to spend the time to think through their operations.

I speak from long experience and from personal failure that came from springing into action before I had done the thinking. I learned this lesson the hard way. I hope to help you avoid having to learn this lesson the hard way.

If cash flow planning is new to you, I recommend that you study the Acme Widgets cash flow budget shown in the Appendix. It will provide you with a template for preparing your own cash flow budget, if you don't already have one. Acme is a relatively simple operation. But its cash flow budget contains a lot of numbers. It takes a lot of thought to come up with a good cash flow budget. Of course, it can be simplified in several ways. You could budget by quarters instead of by the month. You can lump together small items into a single category. And so on.

Beware: budgeting by the year is not detailed enough to be useful. At some point during the year you could be in a negative cash position, even though you begin and end the year in a positive cash position. Without understanding that for a period of time during the year the organization would need to find outside funds, there could be serious problems. What if the end of the month came and there was no money to pay salaries? It would not be of any use to tell employees that over the next few months you expect that there will be enough cash coming in to pay them.

A friend was the chief financial officer of a not-for-profit organization. Going through the finances he was horrified to see that the bank balance did not contain enough cash to meet the next payroll.

Of course, he went to his boss with the bad news. Then the scrambling began. Frantic phone calls were made to past donors to see if they would come up with immediate cash donations. The two organization officers didn't approach the corporations and foundations that provided big money. It would be far too embarrassing to admit the organization had run out of cash.

With a lot of effort, enough money was raised to meet the payroll. Over time, expected payments and grants came in and put the organization into a much better cash position.

But you don't want to repeat that experience. A cash flow budget is the way to prevent that.

In most organizations there is a financial person who will actually prepare the cash flow budget. Other people need to be involved as well, to be sure that the financial person (or whoever is preparing the budget) has all of the necessary information. You don't want to be surprised by something someone in the organization knew about but wasn't asked to reveal.

The annual cash flow budget is the organization's blueprint for the activities of the coming year. It is the plan for what you will be doing.

All of the thinking work you have done will certainly make your organization more likely to be successful. This thinking work has now built a solid foundation for the next Section of this book.

SECTION TWO: DOING TASKS

You have probably accumulated a lot of documents by now, probably both text and spreadsheets. These documents should contain *definitions*, a *mission statement*, *values,* a *vision*, *possible barriers,* a *strategic plan*, and a *budget* for the coming year. It is time to use all that thinking and planning to direct meaningful action. It is time to turn to doing.

Of course, you are already doing. But this section covers a number of specific doing tasks with ideas for accomplishing them more effectively.

A. STAFFING

The first task of doing involves providing the human resources – the people – needed to accomplish the plans. In your strategic planning you should have already set out an organizational plan that defines what staff you will need and when you will need them.

If you are a well-established business, you may have no additional staffing needs. Everyone that is required to operate the organization successfully is already on board. For the coming year, you are in good shape. (But perhaps your strategic plan indicates that more staff will be needed in the future. If so, then this chapter on staffing can be a help for the future.)

1. **Describing the Jobs:**

If you need to recruit staff this activity usually starts with writing a job description for each position you are planning to fill.

The Internet, the library, and bookstores have many resources that tell about writing a good job description. Most of these are aimed at large company needs.

For smaller organizations, the task is simpler. You need to be clear about exactly what skills you need. Then you need to know how much you can pay to acquire a person with those skills (or a person who can quickly learn those skills.) Finally, you must be clear about how you will evaluate job performance. What measures will you use to determine if the job is being done satisfactorily?

In most organizations, the staff is a team. They must work together. Teamwork is critical. So any job description needs to include *"Ability to work as part of the team."*

Here is a brief outline of the items in a job description:
1. Job title.
2. Job activities (what will the person do?)
3. Skills, knowledge, personal qualifications needed.
4. Pay range.
5. Ability to work as part of the team.
6. Measurements that will be used to evaluate performance.

The skills might be mechanical skills such as computer programming or the operation of a certain type of machine. But they might also be interpersonal skills, the ability to work with customers or clients.

Often interpersonal communication capabilities are more important than mechanical skills.

There are many aspects of a job that can be taught – and usually need to be taught. On-the-job training is almost always required. But some things can't be taught. You will not be able to teach good interpersonal skills to a grump. You won't be able to make a team player out of a long-time loner. Your job description needs to identify the key personal characteristics the job requires.

And it should note the skills that can be taught in on-the-job training. (In a small organization, on-the-job training can be a problem, since there may not be anyone who has time to do this with a new employee. Keep this in mind if you have only a few staff.)

It is difficult to come up with objective ways to learn if a person can be a part of your team. But look at their past experiences. Your subjective responses to the person during the interview can also be useful.

Put down the pay range planned for the job.

How will you (or the supervisor) evaluate the person once they are on the job? What measures will determine if they are succeeding or failing? The more objective these are, the better. This is usually the most difficult part of writing a job description. It is the most important!

In today's environment you will need to consider whether the job can be done from home, either full-time or part-time. You are likely to face questions about provisions for child care needs. You should be prepared, in the job description, to answer these issues.

The job description will provide the basis for evaluating candidates. It will serve as a "crib sheet" to use when you interview.

In many organizations it is a supervisor who is responsible for hiring. The supervisor needs to be prepared, just as the leader would be if the leader was doing the hiring. The leader needs to be sure that the hiring supervisor is prepared. A good job description is the start.

Do you have job descriptions for current staff? If not, then you have work to do. It is especially important that the evaluation measures for the jobs of current staff are put down. Otherwise, how will you really know if they are performing as you expect?

2. **Recruiting:**

The first place to begin the hunt for a new employee is with yourself. Who do you know that might become a good member of your team? Who among your friends might be able to recommend someone?

Ask your current staff members to recommend someone to fill the open spot. (But be careful. If someone recommends a brother or sister or a close friend and you turn the person down, this can create a problem. If this happens, you need to be prepared to explain to your staff member exactly why the person they recommended didn't fit.)

You can advertise openings in your local newspaper. And there are several Internet sites that can be used to seek candidates. CraigsList is one that is often used. LinkedIn is another. Monster.com is yet another. There are several others that an Internet search will bring up.

You should ask prospective candidates to provide you with a cover letter that provides basic information. It is often helpful to ask them to provide samples of their work or other written information.

I am not enthusiastic about e-mail applications. I believe you can learn a great deal more about a candidate by receiving a written, mailed response.

For low-level entry jobs, candidates may not be able to provide written documents. Their educational background may not have prepared them to do this well. If the job does not require skills in written communication, then go ahead without them.

In a down economy, you will receive far more responses than you can easily handle. To cut back on the number, you must be quite specific about the skills and experience you seek. Eliminate the many responses that don't fit.

In a booming economy, it is often difficult to get any responses, especially if your organization is small and little known.

In such an economy, the efforts of your own staff or your friends and acquaintances are more likely to be productive.

Once you have responses, you must move quickly to get back to the persons you find interesting. Arrange for them to come to your place of business at a mutually convenient time.

Leaders often ask about recruiting and hiring family members. You should definitely consider family members. They can be the most loyal and the hardest-working employees.

But you should definitely be very careful. A family employee may expect special treatment such as extra time off or higher pay or more authority than is warranted.

You need to be very clear to any family member exactly what the job requires and that you can only consider them if they can do the job. You need to tell them that they will be objectively evaluated just like any other employee. If they are unable to do the job, then you will not be able to keep them on. The dynamics of the extended family can make all this easy or extremely difficult.

You need to give very careful thought to the family situation and to the specific family candidate before you act. Firing a family member is even more difficult than firing another unproductive employee.

Once candidates have been recruited, interviewing comes next.

3. **Interviewing:**

Successful interviewing is one part of successful hiring of successful employees. Successful interviewing requires preparation. In your job description you should have identified the key attributes you seek.

You now need to select three to five of the most important attributes and set up a basis for scoring them. I suggest that you decide on what the "ideal" candidate would have on each attribute. That would get a score of five. A candidate with little or none of that attribute would get a score of one.

An attribute might be past experience in a similar job. It might be the ability operate a machine. It might be a specific educational background. Or perhaps excellent communication skills.

You are setting up a more analytical approach to rating candidates. For example, if previous relevant job experience is a key attribute, then a candidate with lots of such experience would get a five. A candidate with little or no relevant job experience would get a one. Some candidates would fall between.

In this aspect of interviewing you are trying to be as objective as possible, uninfluenced by the candidate's demeanor, dress, etc.

When you have interviewed and scored all of the candidates, you add up the scores for each one. You will now be able to rank the candidates by their score.

Of course, you also want to exercise your personal judgment as a further screen. The top scoring candidate may have left you cold. But don't discard that top scorer until you are sure that your personal feelings should weigh more than their top score.

Much research has shown that subjective interviews are not very effective at choosing good employees. This very simplified more-or-less objective scoring system has proven over and over to produce better results than just depending on your personal impressions.

(Here is another factor: Interviews conducted just before lunch or at the end of the day seem to result in less favorable impressions than interviews conducted first thing in the morning or after lunch.

Why? It seems that as the day goes on and your energy level declines, you tend to view candidates less favorably. After a meal, your energy level goes up and you look more favorably on candidates. You can't always schedule interviews right after you have eaten, but you need to keep this in mind as you review your impressions of candidates.)

In interviewing candidates, you will need to find out if they have the skills you need. This will probably be an item you score. If they only have some of those skills, do you believe their intelligence, attitude, willingness to learn can rapidly give them the full set of skills? Will on-the-job training get the person to the skill level required?

A very important part of the interviewing is to find out if the person is likely to fit well in your organization, with your team. Nowadays, in most smaller organizations (and in many large ones,) a candidate for a position is interviewed by all of the people on the team. The team members then give their evaluations of the candidate to the person doing the actual hiring.

If you are comfortable with the skill set and the personality characteristics, and if the other members of your team approve the candidate, there is a good chance that the candidate will become a good staff member and a productive part of your team.

A critical aspect of your organization is values. Values were addressed in the Thinking Section. You want to evaluate a candidate in terms of how well he or she can accept and foster the organization's values.

If the job involves interaction with customers or clients, good interpersonal skills are more important than other skills, which can usually be learned. In an interview, the candidate for such a job needs to look you in the eye, answer questions with confidence, be comfortable with himself or herself. Do you like the person? If not, then the person probably won't be a good hire for a job that requires interpersonal activity.

You want to look at the person's experiences. Do these indicate perseverance, willingness to work hard, commitment to results? Whether the experiences are only in school or also in other organizations, you can see if the person is likely to be a good, hard-working member of your team.

Explore gaps in schooling or gaps in employment. Why did these happen? Do they seem to indicate lack of perseverance? Or are there good explanations for the gaps?

You need to spend enough time on the interview to feel comfortable that you can make a good decision. If the person being interviewed talks on and on, don't hesitate to cut them off. Sometimes, nervousness leads people to blabber. That can be overlooked. But if the person just likes to talk to hear themselves, that is probably not the kind of person you want.

Unless you are absolutely sure that you have found the right person and fear losing them to another employer, you should not make a hiring decision on the first interview.

If you believe the candidate has a good chance of being a good choice, schedule a second interview where both you and the candidate can dig deeper into the job and the fit.

You have arranged to meet with a candidate or candidates for the position you are trying to fill. Before the actual meetings take place, you need to be prepared. Do you have a clear definition of three to five items you will score? Do you know what attributes will deserve the top score in each item?

Write out a list of the questions you will ask. It is easy to forget to ask important questions in the heat of an interview. Review your job description and have it handy during the interview process to keep the interview focused.

> There are some questions you cannot legally ask. You cannot ask about age, race, ethnicity, gender or sex, country of origin or birthplace, religion, disability, marital or family status, or pregnancy, now or planned. Your employment application form can't ask for these. Nor can these be asked about in an interview.

Of course, you can infer much from what you observe and hear in the interview. But remember, good employees are not distinguished by those characteristics you can't ask about. If a person can do the job well, age, race, ethnicity, and so on really don't matter.

A very important time is when you first meet the candidate. Do they look you in the eye? Give you a strong handshake? Seem comfortable? You can tell a lot by first impressions.

But of course, a job interview is stressful for the applicant. That may cause them to be less impressive than they could be. You need to take that into account. As the interview progresses, you can observe whether or not a tense candidate loosens up, becomes more comfortable and open. And of course, the scoring system is a way for you to get around the candidate's nervousness.

You need to explain what the position entails. What skills are necessary. What interaction with others the job requires. What are the hours? Where will the job take place? You can't cover everything, but you need to be reasonably specific. If the other members of your staff will be interviewing, let the applicant know this.

Then let the candidate talk. Have them tell you about their most recent job experiences, about their educational experiences. Find out about their hobbies, what they do in their time off.

While they are talking you may want to take notes. (But don't concentrate on the note-taking so that the candidate believes you are not really listening.)

You are trying to find out what kind of person the candidate is. To do this, you need to start the conversation with a question or two. But you need to let the candidate talk as much as possible. (In my experience, interviewers often talk too much. They dominate the conversation and thus can learn little from listening. Don't be like that.)

If you are looking for someone to interact with customers or clients, you should be able to tell if the candidate is a good communicator, conveys warmth and enthusiasm, and appears able to interact well with you. You don't want a dour, introverted, uncommunicative person to work with your customers or clients, no matter how many skills and how much experience they have.

If the person is obviously wrong for the job, don't waste too much time on an interview. There will likely be no need to go into pay and benefits. Even as you dismiss the unsuitable candidate, be sure to thank them for giving you their time. Wish them well. The person may be or become a customer or client and you want them to leave with positive feelings, even if you do not offer them a job.

With luck, it will not take too many interviews before you come up with one or more candidates that seem well-suited for the job. If you are going to have your current staff interview them, make arrangements for the candidate's return to accomplish this. You should have told your staff that they will be doing this task. They need to see the job description. You will want to provide them with background on the candidate or candidates so that they are prepared for a productive interview.

After they have interviewed the candidate, you need their feed-back. It is well to have them put this in writing, following a standard format. (You may want them to use the simple scoring system you have devised.)

What strengths did the candidate show? What possible weaknesses did you see? Could you work on a daily basis with this person? What other comments do you have?

After that, you need to move promptly. A good candidate is likely to have other offers.

You will usually have a second interview with someone you want to hire. During this interview you will go over pay and benefits. (And you may need to negotiate these.) To do this well, you need to have a very clear idea of how much you can pay, before the candidate comes back. Don't hem and haw about what you can pay. Be willing to be flexible, within the range you have already established for the job. And remember, one of the more demoralizing things you can do is to pay a new hire more than you are paying the people who are already on your staff doing the same or similar job.

If the position you are hiring for involves the handling of significant amounts of the organization's money, and if you do not know the person well, you should definitely do a background check. It is all too easy to fake a resume, to come across in an interview as a solid candidate for the job, when the real background is one that would definitely make you reject the person. (The Internet will direct you to many sources for background checks.)

Contacting previous employers is seldom very helpful. They will not (and legally cannot) tell you much about the candidate.

After all this, you should have hired the right person for your job opening. But remember, only time will tell if you made a good decision. No interview or even series of interviews can guarantee that the right person has been employed.

All of these steps should be followed by supervisors who do hiring. As the leader, you need to be sure that supervisors understand the process and follow it. They definitely must know what questions they cannot legally ask.

One last thought about choosing a candidate for a job. Good leaders hire people that are smarter and more capable than they are. Poor leaders look for people that are not as smart or capable as they are. Poor leaders are afraid of people brighter than they are. Their ego requires that they have to be the smartest one. But that is not how leaders are successful. Having a staff that is smarter, more knowledgeable, and harder working than the boss is sure to make the boss look good and the organization be successful. When all the staff are dumber than the boss, they cannot make the boss look better than he or she is. They are not likely to build a successful organization.

4. **Mistakes:**

You can never be sure you have chosen the right person. No matter how much time and effort you give to recruiting and interviewing, seeking the right candidate, you may be wrong in your judgment. Over time, the new hire may prove not to be what you expected.

When this happens – and it happens often enough – you need to move quickly. You must judge whether or not you or other members of your team can help the person become the employee you wanted. If you think that the employee could be helped, then go to it. But set a time limit to see if change occurs.

Many organizations hire people on the clear understanding that there will be trial or probationary period. Only after the trial period will the person become a regular employee. The length of the trial period will depend upon the type of job. Simple jobs, short period.

If the person is unlikely to become what you want, or if your efforts to help them change do not work out within the time frame or trial period you have set, then act.

Your action must be to let that employee go. In harsh words, fire them. You can't afford to keep an employee that does not make a strong positive contribution to your organization. A poor employee takes money from the organization without contributing. Having a poor employee on staff keeps you from going out to find an employee who will make a strong positive contribution.

A smaller organization cannot afford to have someone on the team who is not making a strong contribution to the organization's success.

One of the hardest things for a boss to do is to fire someone. One of the worst things a boss can do is to keep a non-performing employee on and on. This demoralizes other members of the team and drags down the performance of your organization. Swallow hard and do what must be done for the good of the organization.

Do it yourself, as pleasantly as you can. I have used these words: "You just didn't seem to fit into our organization in the way that we needed. I am sure you will find another organization that will be a better fit for you…"

Too often I kept on an unproductive employee because I was unwilling to take on the unpleasant task of letting them go. I shied away from confronting the person with bad news. This was one of my worst failings as a boss. And it cost my company money and probably kept us from accomplishing as much as we should have. Don't make those mistakes. Grit your teeth and do what you know must be done.

A common axiom is "Hire slow, fire fast."

5. **<u>Outside Resources:</u>**

There are many specific skill sets that can be obtained from outside sources, on an as-needed, free-lance basis. With the Internet, the persons with these skills need not be close to you. They could be as far away as India, for example. Before you go looking to add an employee ask yourself if your organization would be better off, at least in the short run, engaging an outside person or group to handle a specific task.

This is now very common in the book publishing industry. There are free-lance designers, editors, promotion specialists, sales forces, warehouse and distribution organizations, and so on. With the help of all these outside experts it is possible to be a one-person publishing company. (Of course, a company that publishes many books will surely build its own staff to do these various tasks.)

For smaller organizations I strongly recommend engaging an outside accounting person or organization. There are now so many complex tax requirements from federal, state, and local governments that you need to have an expert in this area to provide advice and to handle the filing of all the required returns and reports. Don't put off engaging this expertise. You don't want to get into difficulties with one or another government entity because you failed to meet a legal requirement.

If you are a start-up, you need this accounting and tax advice from the beginning. It will cost money. But getting into trouble because you didn't know you had to file a report or return will cost a lot more money.

Another piece of advice: You need to think carefully about the legal structure of your organization. Many organizations start as personal (sole) proprietorships. But as you grow, you ought to have an organizational structure that protects you from personal liability and frivolous lawsuits. This could be a corporation – for-profit or not-for-profit. A for-profit corporation can be a C-corporation or an S-corporation. There are LLCs – limited liability companies. Various kinds of partnerships can be set up. You need legal advice to choose the right structure for your operation. Find a good lawyer early on and let the lawyer advise you on how to set up the proper legal organization. This will cost money, but it is money well spent to avoid potential problems.

Various legal web sites offer inexpensive help and forms. But in order to know what is best for your organization and for you, personal legal advice is likely to be better in the long run.

You and other members of the staff are probably very good at some tasks. You are probably less than good at others, perhaps avoiding doing them until the last minute. Identifying these strengths and your weaknesses is important. There may be outside independent individuals or organizations that can provide strength where you are weak. (That is most likely to be accounting and legal.)

There are almost certainly areas in which outside expertise can be of significant benefit.

Many of the skills and much of the specialized knowledge your organization needs can often be found in independent outside organizations or individuals. Your friends and associates and, of course, the Internet, can help you find the outside resources the organization needs.

Once you have recruited, interviewed, and hired the staff your organization needs, there are some important tasks to accomplish.

B. <u>TRAINING</u>

Now that you have hired a person, you can't just say "There's your work station. Go to it." Training is necessary. You or one of your staff should work closely with the new hire, showing them exactly what they need to do in the job. Showing once is not sufficient. All of us need to be told and be shown several times. We all need a more experienced person to look over our shoulder and correct us (nicely) when we go astray at an unfamiliar task. Depending on the job, training may take a week, a month, or even longer.

Whatever the new hire said in the job interview about his or her experiences, you cannot count on past experiences making the person fully capable for the job in your organization.

The job will usually require a specific set of skills. Perhaps the new hire brings these skills to the job. Perhaps the skills need to be taught. The job training certainly must include a focus on the skills needed for success. Often, developing the skills to the right level will take practice. You need to be realistic about the time required to develop the skills that will be needed to do the job effectively.

Sometimes a new employee will come with skills already developed, but applied in the wrong way for your organization. Training needs to address this.

For example a receptionist might have come from an organization that emphasized a terse, business-like approach. If your organization favors a warmer, less formal approach, the new receptionist will need training, even if all the basic skills are there.

During the training, you or the trainer must evaluate the new hire's capabilities. Are they able to learn to handle the job requirements effectively? Is it clear that they will grow into the job and be a strong, positive contributor to the organization's success? If not, perhaps the wrong person was hired.

When you recognize this, you must move promptly to let that person go so that you can then look for a person who will be able to do the job well and help your organization be successful.

Here are some other things that need to be covered in job training. Too often they are not covered.

Working hours – start, finish, breaks, lunch time. If there is a time clock or if time records are kept, the new hire needs to be shown how to deal with these.

Locations – rest rooms, lunch room, parking, bulletin board for notices, and so on. It is a good idea to take a tour of the premises on the first day to orient the new hire to the geography.

Dress code.

Computer systems and their use. (Also telephones.)

What expenses the person may incur on the job and how these will be reimbursed.

If the new hire will be working some or all of the time from home, exactly what reports must they submit? How often will they need to come to the organization's premises?

What to do if sickness or some other issue prevents the person from coming to work.

Introductions – the new hire should be introduced to as many staff members as possible, especially if the person was not interviewed by the team.

Be sure that the person is absolutely clear who their supervisor is. They need to know who to go to when they have questions or if issues come up. The new hire will have many questions, often about matters you take for granted. Be sure they know who to ask and that they feel comfortable about asking.

Anyone who works directly with customers or clients will need to have all of the information required to get their job done. Customers or clients are easily turned off when someone shrugs their shoulders when asked a question and says, "I don't know."

Of course, there will be questions that require the person to say, "That's a question I can't answer; I'll have to get my supervisor (or get back to you) so you can get a definitive answer."

Successful retail operations usually prepare a list of frequently-asked questions with the appropriate replies so everyone interacting with customers is prepared. Organizations where the staff work directly with clients must have a prepared list of the questions and answers that will come up most frequently.

Job training is an important task that is often given short shrift. It shouldn't be. It is a key part of turning a new hire into a successful employee.

If your organization is unwilling to spend the time to fully train new employees, don't expect that they will become good, productive employees. And don't expect to have a really successful organization with poorly-trained employees.

Job training is not a one-time occurrence. It should involve regular coaching, usually as long as an employee is on the job. In team sports, the coach doesn't show a player how to accomplish the task just once. The coach is regularly looking at performance, suggesting improvements, and most important, complimenting improvements and good performance to encourage more of the same.

Your organization needs to make ongoing coaching a regular part of job training.

C.ENCULTURATION

Job training is an important task that must be done with a new employee. But there is another important task.

Your organization has a culture. This is probably not written down, as job descriptions are. But the culture of your organization has a very substantial influence on how things are done and on whether your organization will be successful.

An organization's culture might be compared to the water in which fish live. Fish do not think about the water as they swim. It is just there, a part of their environment they need not pay much attention to. Except when the water changes. A cod, used to swimming in cold, clear, salt water will not fare well in warm, muddy, fresh water. On the other hand, a catfish used to swimming in warm, muddy, fresh water would not fare well in cold, clear, salt water.

You and your employees are living and working in a certain culture. It seems a natural part of the environment. You probably don't give it much thought.

But a new employee, coming from a different culture, will notice the differences and will be uncomfortable if the differences are too great from the culture previously experienced.

Most people are malleable enough so that they can adapt to your organization's culture. But if they get active help, they will understand the culture and become a part of it quickly.

Enculturation is the fancy word that characterizes the process. You, your supervisors, and other employees need to help the new employee quickly understand and accept the culture of your organization.

What is the culture of your organization?

You may never have given this conscious thought. Now you need to do this. And if the culture within your organization is not effectively working to support the mission then you should work to change the culture. Cultures get deeply ingrained, and only much effort over a long period of time is likely to bring about a major shift in the culture of your organization.

Let me suggest some kinds of cultures. You can think which, if any, of these describe your organization's culture.

There is the pyramid culture. A strong leader at the top, subservient supervisors below, and interchangeable peons at the bottom. In such a culture, fear of the powerful boss is often a controlling factor.

I don't believe this top-down, fear-based culture is really effective in the current environment. Young people have generally not been raised or educated in such a setting, and they usually rebel if put into such an organization. This makes for an unstable work force that seldom puts the organization's needs first.

In such an organization employees seldom make decisions on their own. Even if a decision is needed right away, they will pass the buck up the line in order to avoid responsibility.

Another type of culture emphasizes hierarchy, bureaucracy, structure, and standards. This type of culture is common in government agencies. In a stable environment, this cultural model works reasonably well. It attracts employees who want the structure. Such an organization, however, finds it difficult to cope with rapid change.

If your organization must deal with a constantly shifting environment, this is probably not an effective culture. If your organization is in a stable environment where precisely following government, foundation, or major customer mandates is critical, then a culture modeled on government bureaucracies can work well. Not every potential employee will find such a culture to their liking. Over time, your staff will sort out so that employees comfortable with this kind of culture make up the bulk of the work force.

Another kind of culture is project or task oriented. In such a culture, the work force is often organized into teams that tackle a project. When the project is finished, the teams break up and are reassembled to work on new projects. This culture is common in software companies. To be successful, the project or task has to be clearly defined, the team leader carefully chosen, and regular oversight of progress is necessary.

Most young people today have been working in teams since they began their schooling. They are comfortable in such a culture. (Older leaders may not be aware of how team-oriented young people are.)

The speed at which the organization's activities must take place is another factor characterizing cultures. In a restaurant everything must move at high speed during meal times. An employee who is not comfortable with a high-speed culture is likely to not fit in and stay for long.

The attitude toward risk is another factor that characterizes a culture. Some organizations are doing well-defined tasks with clear parameters. The risks are low. This suits persons who are normally risk-averse.

In other organizations, there is a high risk of failure (but there are usually large rewards when success occurs.) In such an organization, failures occur and are accepted. But failures are learning experiences that help to avoid the same kind of failure in the future.

If your organization needs its employees to take risks, then you have to accept some failures. Chewing out or firing employees who try hard, do their best, yet still suffer failure on a project or task will not support an effective risk-taking culture.

There are other aspects of culture. Is yours a formal organization where employees address you (especially) by title and hesitate to come directly to you with a problem?

Or do you have an informal culture, where everyone is on a first-name basis, and the chain of command is less rigorous?

There are two very important factors that affect the culture of an organization.

First are the values of the organization. The culture must support the values. The values must support the culture.

In the chapter on values, you read that one of the values I had developed was "The customer comes first!" If that is an important value, then the culture must support it. Employees need to feel empowered to deal directly with customer concerns. If they don't put the customer first then the culture and the values are not in congruence. (And you need to ask, why not? Perhaps you say that the customer comes first, but in practice, that is not what happens when profits might be affected.)

A major aspect of enculturating new employees will be educating them on the values of the organization. This is a part of the training for new employees. It directly affects how quickly a new employee will become part of your organization's culture.

The second important factor that affects the culture is what you measure and reward. Employees will be well aware of what aspects of their work you (and their supervisors) will measure. If rewards (praise, raises, recognition) are closely tied to what is measured then you can be sure that the culture of your organization is shaped by what is measured and what is rewarded.

Take some time to think about the kind of culture your organization has. Is it the kind you want? The kind that will produce the greatest chance of success? If you have a culture that isn't working very well to help achieve the organization's mission, then you have some work to do.

A new employee needs to understand and adapt to the culture of your organization – become enculturated. If your employees see and understand the culture differently than you do, you can be sure that a new employee will be at first confused and will then adapt to the employee-fostered culture.

"Yeah, the boss says he wants us to put customers first. He keeps harping on that as a key value. But then if you do something for a customer that costs money or that doesn't work out, you can count on getting chewed out. So keep you head down and follow the manual…"

Be sure that your values and your culture are the ones that the current employees buy into. Then they will help a new employee to understand and accept these values and the culture.

Management experts agree that a strong culture that permeates the organization leads to strong organizational performance. So work at enculturation just as you work at training.

A last word: Staff failures are almost always *leadership* failures. The wrong person was hired. The new hire was poorly trained. The person was never helped to adapt to the culture. The person was not clearly informed about the job requirements or the evaluation measures. And so on. If you chose a new hire who didn't work out, you need to think carefully about where *you* failed, about what you could have done differently, and how you will avoid those mistakes in the future. If your supervisors are consistently hiring the wrong person, you need to be sure that your leadership of the supervisors has the right focus.

D. <u>DIRECTING</u>

Employees without clear direction cannot be expected to work effectively to achieve the mission of the organization.

Directing is not just saying "Do this." Then, "Do that." And so on. You have better uses for your time than constantly directing each employee's activities. And employees do not appreciate nagging.

Neither you nor your supervisors can oversee everything. The most effective direction comes when employees are self-directing. Self-direction is much more powerful than any directions you or your supervisors can give. Good hiring, good training, and good enculturation will help give your organization self-directing employees.

Employees exercise self-direction because they have a clear understanding of the organization's mission, values, goals, and plans. They support these in their work. Employees who understand their job requirements can self-direct. And motivation is the key to self-direction.

After a new employee has been trained and made comfortable in your culture, then there should be no need for anyone to constantly look over that employee's shoulder to see that he or she is doing the job. Of course, you and your supervisors need to be good coaches. You want to help each employee, old or new, to regularly improve job performance. That help will occur occasionally. But most of the time, neither you nor your supervisors will be watching over an employee. Employees need to be self-directing most of the time.

Why would an employee take personal responsibility for working toward the organization's goals?

Because that employee has a clear understanding of what his or her part is in achieving organizational success. You have made sure that they are well-trained and have become comfortable with the culture of the organization. You have made them a part of your team and they feel that they are a part of the team. They take personal responsibility for team success. Being part of a team is a powerful motivator.

Finally, you have made clear their authority and their responsibility. You don't want to have employees constantly coming to ask if they have the authority to do this or that. You want them to know what they are responsible for and what you expect from them.

Self-motivated and self-directed employees who belong to a team are the employees who will best move the organization toward accomplishment of its mission.

You need to be sure that all of the employees are familiar with the mission, the values, and the annual plan. They need to know where the organization is going. Then they need to know what their part is in getting the organization there.

That means clear, specific directions about what to do, when to do it, and *why* to do it. Effective directions are given one-on-one. They are presented both orally and in writing so that there is no misunderstanding. But once those directions have been given, employees are likely to be mostly on their own to achieve results.

If you have an employee who constantly needs direction, who won't do anything without having a supervisor specifically tell the employee what to do, then you have the wrong employee.

Your write-up of the evaluation measures for the job will help you or your supervisors give effective directions. Employees need to be clear about how they will be measured. You need to be clear about how you will measure them. When employees are clear about how their job performance will be measured, they can then self-direct their efforts toward meeting those evaluation measures.

As noted in the section on job descriptions, writing down clear and useful evaluation measures is not easy. But the time spent to think through evaluation will pay off in a major way. When both the boss and the employee clearly understand how a job will be evaluated, they have a mutual focus. The employee can be self-directing, knowing what the objectives are. The boss need not constantly oversee the employee.

When you hire a new employee you should always ask yourself, "Can he or she become self-directing? Or will we have to be constantly looking after that employee?"

You may have an employee who does not take responsibility for accomplishing the job. This employee may seem to need constant direction from you or the supervisor. Or it may be the employee has not become a team member. Despite your efforts, this employee seems unable to fit into your organization.

One of the worst mistakes that a boss can make is to keep such an employee on. Sometimes the boss hopes that further nagging will turn the employee around. Sometimes the boss is just unwilling to grab the bull by the horns and fire the employee.

The other members of the team will certainly know if the organization has an employee that is not carrying his or her part of the load. Their morale and spirit will not be helped by seeing a non-performer stay on the payroll.

So take action when it is clear that the person does not fit and cannot become a productive team member contributing to the organization's success.

Discharging such a person provides an opportunity to find another person who can measure up, who can become a real contributor to the success of the organization.

(But remember: an employee who does not work out usually indicates that the person doing the hiring or supervising failed in some way.)

Every person in the organization needs to have a clear understanding of the organization's mission. Every person needs a clear understanding of what they must do to contribute to accomplishing the mission. Everyone must understand the values that should guide their actions. Leaders provide direction that makes employees self-directing in their daily activities.

Of course, you can't assume that every employee will effectively self-direct to achieve the organization's goals. There needs to be regular evaluation and then, regular feedback to the employee. Often a friendly nudge will get things on track. Or perhaps more extensive coaching for a period of time will turn things around.

Hiring the right people is the most important part of directing. If you don't have the right people in your organization, self-direction to achieve the organization's goals is unlikely. If you have an employee that requires constant overseeing, then you probably hired the wrong person. (Or the training of this person was poorly done. If better training will turn the employee around, give it a try.)

You cannot watch over every employee every hour of the day. You must have employees who self-direct with full understanding of the mission, values, plans, and how what they do fits into the team's overall work.

The leader needs to decide how the job will be evaluated, then work very hard to hire the right person. Then see that appropriate training and enculturation occur. Evaluation must be done regularly with feedback to the employee. And coaching will be given as required.

Starting with the right person is the most important part of the process.

Delegation: In every organization of any size, the leader must delegate responsibility and authority to others. Once the number of employees gets up to a certain number – ten is often considered to be the number – then it is not possible for the leader to direct them all, even with good self-direction. The span of control has become too wide. If the organization is to be successful, the leader must delegate.

Delegation is based on trust. To give someone responsibility and authority over an area of the organization's operations, and over other employees, you must trust the person you name. You must trust that they will take on the responsibility. You must trust that they will use the authority wisely.

As Ronald Reagan said about dealing with the Soviets, "Trust, but verify." No matter how much you trust the person you have delegated responsibility and authority to, you need to verify that they are doing the job effectively.

That doesn't mean hovering over them, checking every day, every hour. But it does mean regularly assessing performance.

Both you and the person you delegate authority and responsibility to must be clear on how the job will be evaluated.

The person you delegate to become a supervisor of aspects of your operations should not be chosen on the basis of personal likes. The choice should be made because the person seems to be the most qualified to supervise. And not everyone is qualified.

Many people do not want to take on the job of overseeing others. Telling others what to do, perhaps even having to fire someone, is something that many people shy away from. Such people seldom make good supervisors.

On the other hand, some people become tyrants when given authority over others. They are overbearing supervisors who often drive away good employees.

> Research shows that employees usually quit because of a bad relationship with their supervisor, not because of the job or the organization.

I have appointed supervisors who seemed to me just right. Their interactions with me were excellent – friendly but business-like. But I found out from walking around that they put on an entirely different face when dealing with their subordinates. They became nasty dictators. The way such supervisors deal with the boss is entirely different than the way they deal with subordinates. And they cause serious trouble in an organization.

You need to watch out for this two-faced characteristic when you have delegated responsibility and authority. One measure to watch for is employee turnover. A supervisor whose employees are constantly turning over is not doing a good job for the organization.

But delegate you must when your organization is too large for you to personally direct each employee.

When you delegate, you need to carefully and clearly outline the exact responsibilities you are delegating. What will the supervisor be responsible for? What will you measure them on? Once again, a clear definition of evaluation measures is critical.

You need to be equally careful and clear about the authority you are delegating. Does it include the authority to hire? To fire?

When will the supervisor need to come to you for approval of actions or initiatives?

If you have chosen well and made the responsibility and authority clear, it is likely that your organization's operations will become much more effective. And you will be a more successful leader.

You certainly won't be able to grow effectively without delegation. Do it well.

E. <u>CONTROLLING</u>

You are the boss. That means you have ultimate control over the organization's results (and the ultimate responsibility.) To have ultimate control, you need to take various controlling actions.

Good controlling is a process that builds and supports employee self-direction, while ensuring that the organization achieves its goals.

"Controlling" has a negative connotation. Here is what it means in the context of leadership.

You need to regularly and frequently compare actual results with planned results. In most organizations this is done monthly. (But some operations may require weekly or even daily reports of results to compare with planned results for that period.)

You have an annual budget. This should have been broken down into monthly (or more frequent) segments. Now you get regular reports on the activities of your organization. These reports should include all of the items that are in your budget.

Now you can compare what actually happened with what you had planned to happen. There will not be a perfect match. You operate in an imperfect and complex world. It is impossible to plan for the future so that when the future happens it agrees exactly with what you planned. But you hope to be close.

Look at each item, comparing it with your plan. Where there are serious discrepancies, you need to find out the cause. When you find out the cause, this may direct you to take action.

Sometimes revenues will come in higher than you budgeted. This is welcome news. But you want to know why. Did you gain new customers or clients? Did existing customers or clients spend more during the period? Did some delinquent accounts get collected? Find out the reasons for more revenues coming in. Perhaps you need to revise your budget. Or perhaps the coming period will show reduced revenues if you received payments early. Reduced revenues in the next period might cause cash flow problems. You need to look ahead.

If revenues came in less than you had planned that will require some serious investigation. Is this a one-time hit that will be made up in the future? Or did you lose an important customer or client? Are payments coming in more slowly than you planned? Are you going to be below the planned revenues for the rest of the year or will revenues pick up and put your organization back on track? If the organization is going to be below its planned revenues for the future, what does that mean for cash flow? Are there cash flow problems coming up that have to be dealt with?

What are the steps that you need to take to get the cash flow positive in the coming months?

These are tough questions that require hard decisions. And that's what leaders get paid for.

Similar questions will arise as you compare the actual expenditures with the planned expenditures. If the organization spent more than was planned, that leads to tough questions about future spending and cash requirements.

If the organization spent less than planned that may be good news. But it also may be bad news if the reduced spending came about because a key vacancy couldn't be filled, or if shortages made it impossible to buy the goods needed for future sales. You need to analyze why spending went up or why spending went down. Then you need to decide how to adjust the plan and the operations for the future.

Controlling then, involves comparing what was planned with what actually happens and then making adjustments that the actual results indicate. This is not just your task alone. I hope you prepared the annual budget with the deep involvement of all of your staff who are involved in creating revenues or making expenditures.

I hope you are now involving these staff members in analyzing the actual results. You need their input to decide what changes may be necessary in the operations and in the plan.

If things haven't gone as well as planned, this is not the time for the blame game. It is time to get everyone involved in identifying and correcting the problem. Of course, if things have gone better than planned, then congratulations are in order. And then analysis is needed to see what changes may be needed for the future.

How often do you sit with the team to compare actual results with the plan? Some organizations do this daily. In one organization the leader has a conference call with key supervisors, every afternoon at 3:00 PM. The supervisors are scattered around large premises. But they all get on the call at 3:00. Any problems are brought up and someone must commit right then to resolve the problem.

Other organizations have weekly meetings. Probably most assemble the team once a month to compare actual with planned results. These meetings are not just to provide information. Where there is an issue, it must be decided *what* steps will be taken to resolve the issue, *who* will take the responsibility, and *when* action will take place.

The leader makes the assignments and then follows up to be sure things are going as expected. The issue will be brought up at the next meeting and the person who was assigned the responsibility will report. When a person given a responsibility has to report before his or her peers, as well as the leader, this is a powerful motivator.

You are likely not preparing your own reports. Be sure that whoever is preparing these does so in a clear and concise way. If you can't fully understand the reports you can't effectively control. I have often had to work with accounting people to guide them to prepare reports that were most meaningful for me and for other non-accounting people.

A major issue for many organizations is that the key financial reports take so long to be prepared that actions to address problems are taken too late. I have had this problem in several organizations. Sometimes, a new financial person had to be hired. Sometimes the financial report preparation had to be handed over to a more effective outside group. If your financial reports are not timely you cannot control effectively. Take action if your reports come too late to help you control.

Comparing actual results to planned results and then taking needed corrective actions is a major aspect of controlling. You can't manage what you don't measure. But by no means is it the only part of the leader's controlling activities.

The leader of an organization must walk around. That means getting out of the office and away from the desk regularly to be a visible presence where the operations are actually taking place. If the organization has one location, walk around every day.

If the organization is far-flung, then schedule trips to the other locations so you can walk around there. You ought do this as often as you can. Perhaps bi-weekly or once a month if the other locations are close by. Less often, if you need to take an overnight trip. In any case, leaders who stay in their offices are seldom able to exercise wise and effective control.

What do you do when you walk around? You absolutely do not bypass supervisors to give orders or directions. If you see something that needs fixing, you talk to the supervisor in charge, Don't bypass the chain of command. That creates a situation where line workers feel free to bypass their supervisors and come directly to you. That is bad for the supervisors, bad for you, and bad for the organization's functioning.

What you are doing as you walk around is observing and listening. You are likely to see things or to hear comments that will give you a much better understanding of the operations. You ought to be able to gain a feel for morale. You should see whether things seem to be running smoothly or if there are people sitting around waiting for work to flow from somewhere else. There is a great deal to be learned by keeping your eyes and ears open.

Stops on a walk-around always include the rest rooms and the lunch area. If these are clean and neat, this is a good sign. If they are dirty, messy, and poorly maintained, you can be sure that employees were complaining to one another. This is not good for morale and team spirit.

So get out of the office to see and hear what is happening. You do this so you can make better decisions about what changes may be needed to improve operations and results.

When you see a significant issue, then you talk to the person in charge. Is that person aware of the issue? What steps are being taken to deal with it? Is it a broader issue that needs to involve more people? Or have you exaggerated the issue's significance?

In a very small organization, the issue may be your problem. Once you recognize it, fix it. Problems left to fester are the cause of long-term grief.

Leaders must meet with customers or clients. This should be done on a regular basis, just as with the walk-around. You listen, having encouraged the customers or clients to tell you their experiences, impressions, and feelings about the activities of your organization. You ask how they might be served better in the future. A great many of the most important innovations have come from customer or client suggestions.

Of course, your front-line people are talking with customers or clients regularly. Your employees can tell you much during the walk-around. But there is no substitute for the direct connection between the leader and customers or clients. Take the time, make the effort to do this.

This is a good place to talk about trust. You cannot be everywhere, see everything, know everything that is going on in your organization when it gets beyond one or two people in size. You have to trust that the people in the organization are working effectively to achieve the goals that have been set.

You trust people when they have earned that trust, by showing commitment to results, willingness to work as part of a team, and the capability to perform effectively in their job. Once you have developed a soundly-based trust in an employee, your control activities become much easier.

Trust is a two-way street. If your staff do not trust you, the organization is in trouble. You must also earn trust. You need to show your commitment to the organization and to achieving the results you have planned.

If you make a promise, you keep that promise. If you make a mistake, you admit the mistake and set it right. You are firm and consistent in dealings with employees, and others involved with the organization. You are honest and honorable. You live the values.

And then you will have earned the trust of those you deal with. Because of their trust in you, they will follow your leadership with confidence.

When you have built that kind of trust, controlling the organization is a far easier task.

As you can see, controlling means keeping on top of what is happening in the organization, from direct observation as well as from reports, and then taking the actions needed to deal with problems or to adjust to greater success than had been planned on.

Good controlling is subtle. It is constant. It recognizes and deals with change. It helps employees take responsibility and be self-motivated and self-directed – in fact, self-controlled. It is built on mutual trust.

An effective leader is an effective controller.

F. <u>THE GREAT CIRCLE</u>

The path of leadership tracks a great circle. Call it the leadership mandala. In Asian cultures, the mandala is a circle that represents the flow of life. The leadership mandala is a circle that represents the flow of leadership activities.

We began with thinking tasks. Defining products or services, defining customers or clients, defining the benefits that the customers or clients want, defining core competencies, and defining what the leader or leaders want.

These definitions led to the mission statement. Then the values needed to achieve the mission had to be identified. A five-year vision was created. From the vision came a five-year strategic plan. And finally came the plans and budget for the current year. Each thinking task led to the next.

These thinking tasks then led to the doing tasks. These tasks included staffing, training, enculturation, directing, and controlling.

Out of these doing tasks, especially controlling, comes information that leads back to the thinking tasks. What has been learned from the organization's operations that might require redefining products, services, customers, or customer wants?

Perhaps some products are selling more poorly than you thought they would. Perhaps others have done much better. Perhaps clients are demanding more of one kind of service, less of another kind. This may lead to a different mix of products or services being offered.

Perhaps customers or clients that seemed to be the best source of business have proved a disappointment. Perhaps unexpected groups have become important customers.

You and your staff should have been asking customers or clients what they want from your organization. Perhaps what you originally defined as the key want is no longer important to customers or clients. If so, what wants are customers or clients putting at the top of their list?

You may need to work on the definitions in light of what you have learned from operations.

Hopefully, your mission statement was written so that it can accommodate some changes in the definitions. But it is always wise to consider the mission statement at least annually. Is it still a valid statement that attracts?

Are your values understood and operative?

What about the vision? Has your five-year goal been impacted by current activities? Are there new opportunities or new barriers that need to be considered in the vision?

Have barriers arisen that must be tackled? Will they require altering the vision?

Rework the vision if you need to, based on what you have learned from operations.

Then of course if the vision is altered, the strategic plan must be altered.

And finally, the current year's plan may need to be updated in light of what is actually happening on a day-to-day basis.

So *doing* leads back to *thinking*. And that rethinking leads back to doing – to your operations.

The leadership mandala shown on the next page, repeated from the title page and cover, is a very simplified visual representation of this great circle, thinking, to doing, back to thinking. This visual representation is another way to help you see the flow of leadership.

The Leadership Mandala

S W O T ANALYSIS

The letters stand for *Strengths, Weaknesses, Opportunities, Threats.* One of the most useful team thinking tasks is to do a SWOT analysis of the organization.

What are the organization's strengths that it can build upon? What are its weaknesses that will impede success?

What opportunities does the organization have to move forward? What threats are out there that might derail the organization's plans?

You can do your own SWOT analysis. But the analysis becomes much more useful when it is a team effort. Members of the team may recognize strengths you didn't know about. Or they may see weaknesses in the daily activities you are unaware of. Additional viewpoints will likely bring out opportunities or threats that you hadn't thought about.

Who should be on the analysis team? That depends, of course, on the size and make-up of the organization. For a small organization, I would recommend inviting every person on the staff to participate in the SWOT analysis. Just being part of the team for this important task will provide many lasting benefits. (You will show your confidence in them which will build their trust in you.)

A few tools are helpful. The analysis needs at least half a day, and often longer, to be done well. It should be conducted in a room that is comfortable. Participants need to be able to have paper and pen/pencil to write down their thoughts. In front of the room there needs to be a place where ideas can be written down for all to see. Perhaps it will be on a blackboard or whiteboard. Perhaps on a large pad of paper or an easel.

Someone needs to be appointed as the recorder – not the boss! This person will write down on the board or easel the ideas that the group throws out.

Go through each category – strengths first. The procedure will be to have each person call out what they think are the strengths of the organization. These are written down by the recorder. There is no discussion at this point. The idea is to get as many ideas put down as the group can come up with. The leader must squelch any criticism at this point in the process. The leader must encourage everyone to participate.

After strengths, do the same with weaknesses. Some people like to also do opportunities and threats. I have found it useful to work on the strengths and weaknesses of the organization before going on. This means looking first at the strengths that have been recorded.

The participants have to choose the top three, four, or five strengths. There should be discussion. There will be disagreement. The leader moderates and must be sure that everyone has a chance to be heard without interruption. Then, the leader must see that everyone makes their choices.

This is often done by handing out stickers, stars perhaps, or Post-It notes. Each participant goes up to the board or easel and puts three, four, or five stickers alongside his or her top choices for strengths. (If there are a lot of entries to choose from, five should be chosen by each person. With a smaller number, three works better.) When each participant has done this, it is immediately clear which strengths have the most stickers and have been identified as the top strengths of the organization by the group.

(These strengths ought have a close relationship to the core competencies you have identified. If not, then either the identified core competencies or the identified strengths probably need revision. I think this process of identifying organizational strengths is probably the most definitive.)

Repeat the process with weaknesses.

Then go on to opportunities, recording the ideas of everyone on what opportunities the organization has to become more successful. Then apply the stickers to identify what the group believes are the top opportunities.

Do the same process with threats.

There needs to be discussion, perhaps after each category, and certainly at the end. How does the organization capitalize more effectively on the strengths the group has chosen?

What can the organization do to minimize the weaknesses that have been identified?

Discuss the opportunities. Are they within the mission of the organization? Can they be realized with the resources available? Will pursuit of the opportunities interfere with other ongoing activities? Is this a problem or not? The discussion will provide everyone with much greater understanding and point the organization in productive directions.

Then discuss the threats. How can these be countered? What steps need to be taken to mitigate the threats. Do any of the threats have the potential to kill the organization? How can such fatal threats be averted? Again, the discussion will provide the participants with much greater understanding and point toward ways to overcome or avoid threats to the organization.

The SWOT analysis can be a useful activity to undertake prior to going through the thinking tasks – reviewing products and services, customers or clients, and benefits provided to them – reviewing the mission, the vision, and updating the strategic plan and annual budget.

The strengths, weaknesses, opportunities, and threats that have been identified are very valuable guidelines in the review of these thinking tasks.

The SWOT analysis sometimes turns up new issues and ideas. But most of the time, it brings into the open issues and ideas that most people are aware of but have not really focused on. The SWOT analysis procedure brings the ideas and issues into focus, allows them to be given serious attention, and usually leads to better plans and outcomes.

One way to begin the process is to do your own SWOT analysis. Give yourself several hours and focus your attention on each of these items – strengths, weaknesses, opportunities, and threats to the organization. Put down your own thoughts. How do these alter your perceptions and your ideas about what the organization needs to do?

Having tried out the process for yourself, then you want to do it with your team. But do not put your ideas out there to dominate the team's thinking. Let them get their ideas recorded and the top three, four, or five chosen in each category. I believe you will find that the team's thoughts will be very similar to yours.

You want the team to make their ideas the driving force, not your ideas. They will buy into what needs to be done much more if they see the ideas as their own, not imposed from the top down. It sometimes takes great will power not to dominate the process so that your ideas get top ranking. Leadership is most often listening.

It is possible that the team will go far off base so that a way must be found to get them back on track (and more in tune with the ideas you have developed.) Doing this without turning off the team's enthusiasm and commitment takes a very subtle and low-key approach.

" I wonder if anyone thought about this…?" "Did we miss something…?" "This was hinted at but perhaps didn't get the attention it deserved…" and so on. These are the kind of words I have found useful when I am trying to steer the team away from a dead end and toward more productive avenues of thought. Be non-prescriptive, ask questions rather than imposing conclusions.

Remember, you want the team to wholeheartedly buy into the conclusions so that when you aren't there to oversee the team, they will be self-directed, based on their clear understanding of where the organization needs to go.

SWOT analysis is one of the very valuable thinking tasks that every organization needs to do.

A final word of caution: Luck plays a large part in what happens to any organization. By definition, luck is an "unknown unknown" that happens unexpectedly. Luck can be good or bad. It can't be identified in the SWOT analysis. But it will happen.

That doesn't mean that the thinking tasks and the SWOT analysis are useless. Good luck seems to come most often to those who are prepared. Bad luck is most easily dealt with by those who are prepared. Do the thinking, build a sound organization, and luck will most often be your ally.

COSTS vs. BENEFITS

There is another kind of analysis that is always useful – cost-benefit analysis. This is usually used for analyzing potential projects such as new products or services, potential investments in equipment, or other potential developments within the organization.

A business is considering going into a new product line. What costs will be involved?

These might include the costs of acquiring the inventory, the costs of promoting and marketing the new line, any costs required to provide additional space or equipment, the costs to handle orders and collections, and of course, the costs of any additional employees required.

These costs for the new venture can all be reasonably well projected. But of course, the benefits must also be assessed.

How many units will the new product line sell? How many dollars of sales will come in to cover the costs? Usually, a new product line starts slowly. The start-up costs far outweigh the first year income. So over how long a period should the income from the new product line be projected?

Over one year, usually the costs will be high, the benefits low. What about over five years? Will the projected benefits over the five-year period exceed the costs over that period – exceed them by enough to warrant going forward?

(Beyond five years, almost all projections become guesses and shouldn't guide decisions. Of course, there are projects – developing a new offshore oil field – where the benefits can only cover the costs over a very long period. But smaller organizations seldom have such considerations.)

A non-profit organization sees an opportunity to serve a new group of disadvantaged clients. It will take an investment in equipment, space, and new employees to provide the service. There will be a variety of start-up costs.

The costs can be projected out for five years. The number of clients to be served can be projected. Where will the revenues come from to cover those costs (and provide a reasonable surplus to protect against unforeseen occurrences?)

The benefits to the potential clients can be envisioned. But if there are not financial benefits to the organization that will cover the costs and produce a surplus within a reasonable time period, then the new service should not be undertaken.

Will there be grants, contracts, client payments, and so on to cover the costs? Will the financial benefits to the organization exceed the costs it would incur if it proceeded with the new service? Over how long a time can the organization wait for the financial benefits to offset the costs?

You should to do a cost-benefit analysis with any new project or investment that you are considering for the organization. Often leaders go forward with new projects or investments on the basis of hunches or the feeling that the proposed undertaking can't help but succeed.

"It seems just right for us." "It will really take off and put us far ahead of our competitors." "This will really remake our organization." And so on.

These are the kind of things leaders say about proposed new projects or investments when they don't really want to do the hard work of cost-benefit analysis.

And far too often, projects or investments made without rigorous cost-benefit analysis turn out to be losers, a drag on the organization, and an impediment to the ongoing activities that built the organization's success in the first place.

To grow successfully, you should do cost-benefit analysis on any proposed project or investment that will have a significant effect upon the organization.

The cost-benefit analysis can then be factored into your overall planning as outlined in Section One. The cash flow budget can be revised to show the costs and reflect the benefits.

Cost-benefit analysis has three components: the *costs* that will be incurred, the *benefits* that will accrue, and the *time period* over which the analysis will be done. Each component must be carefully thought-out.

Cost-benefit analysis is a projection of the future. This makes it uncertain and subject to our human failings. If the project is your "baby" it will be difficult for you to make an objective judgment about it. Your own ego will have become invested in the project and this will cloud your ability to make a rational judgment. That is what boards are for. Your board, if you have one, should be asked to review and approve any project that you personally champion.

If the project "belongs" to someone else in your organization, then you will have to provide the thoughtful review that determines if the costs are too low, or the benefits too optimistic, or the time to success too long.

Enthusiasm is necessary for any project to succeed, but enthusiasm can also make us more optimistic than is justified. Cost-benefit analysis needs to balance enthusiasm with objectivity.

A more rigorous but much more valuable way to do a cost-benefit analysis is to look at several possible outcomes. There is the worst case (costs far higher than projected, benefits far lower than projected.) There is the best-guess case (costs and benefits accurately projected over a reasonable time period.) Then there is the best case (costs perhaps much lower or benefits perhaps much higher than projected.)

I recommend that you always force project decisions to consider at least these three possibilities. You and the other participants in the analysis should independently put down your estimate of the odds of each case occurring.

(For example: you might put down "worst case = 20% likelihood, best-guess case = 65%, best case = 15%." The odds need to add up to 100%.)

Then look at the odds each person has predicted. Ask for an explanation of any outliers. (Worst case = 75%, for example.) With the generally-agreed-upon odds in mind, you and the group can make a better decision about whether to move forward on the project.

It is important to consider the worst case. What if that happened? Would it sink the organization? How could the organization cope with a worst-case outcome? Those "unknown unknowns" are out there, waiting to bite. The more complex the project is, the more likely that something will go wrong along the way. Many such problems are temporary glitches, easily handled. But some will kill the project and all the costs incurred will go down the drain.

Optimism is needed to have the confidence to undertake new projects where both costs and benefits occurring in the future are uncertain. But optimism needs to be tempered with a realistic assessment of the potential for unexpected and unwelcome surprises.

Cost-benefit analysis doesn't seem to play a part with some kinds of projects. There are examples of projects, often coming out of Silicon Valley, that seemed almost sure to fail, yet where success brought huge rewards. Venture capitalists invest in high-risk projects knowing that most will fail. But the one that hugely succeeds will make up for many losers.

Most organizations can't afford to have a lot of losers in the hope of one big success. For most organizations cost-benefit analysis is a valuable process.

Make cost-benefit analysis another leadership tool you use. And be sure to consider the worst case and its potential impact on the organization.

THE BEST TEAM WINS

Organizations are made up of people. When people work together as a team, good things happen. And the best team wins.

You are the leader of a team. If you were the coach of a football team and the players were untrained, unmotivated, unfocused, your team would not win. You wouldn't be much of a coach if your team was like that.

If you were the coach of a basketball team where everyone wanted to shoot the ball and no one wanted to pass to another player in better position to score, your team would not win. You wouldn't be much of a coach if your team was like that.

Successful organizations are team efforts where the leader works very hard to build and maintain a great team. Great leaders have great teams. Poor leaders have poor teams.

In the section on doing you have read about staffing, training, enculturation, directing, and controlling. These are vital aspects of developing a winning team. Let me touch on staffing again.

You cannot have a winning team without good members on the team. With the right people on the team, winning comes easily. With the wrong people, even one or two bad apples, it is almost impossible to have a winning team. An indispensable task of leadership is to see that the right people are on the team. Great leaders work hard to staff their team with "stars."

The right people will have enthusiasm, competence, motivation, and the willingness to be contributing members of the team. You can always provide more training, coaching, and supervision to overcome lack of knowledge. You cannot provide more commitment. If you have the wrong people on your team you will not have a winning team.

117

There are some other factors that are important in building and maintaining a winning team. We'll cover those in the remainder of this chapter. But remember, none of these factors are as important as having a team of "stars." Building such a team is THE primary task of the leader.

Here is an aside for the solo entrepreneur reading this book. Research on start-ups has shown that solo entrepreneurs are much more likely to fail than teams of entrepreneurs. You may be the smartest person in the world, but it is very difficult to build a successful organization by yourself.

You need a partner; in fact, two or three partners are even better.

A team will bring together different personalities, different backgrounds, different experiences. When these come together the team will always provide more knowledge, more wisdom, more energy, and more success than a lone ranger can ever provide.

If you are starting an organization, be sure you enlist a team to make it successful.

I worked with a school principal in one of the worst neighborhoods in a very large city. The students in his school outperformed those in schools in far better neighborhoods. He had built a dedicated teaching staff, had enlisted parents, many of them single mothers with little education of their own. The school was neat with no graffiti in a graffiti-smeared area. The sense of "team" was palpable in that school.

I knew he had to cope with rigid union rules, with a distant and overbearing district bureaucracy, with a crime-ridden, dysfunctional neighborhood. And yet he had a high-performance team producing results no one could rightly expect.

By union rules, when an opening occurred in a school in a more desirable neighborhood, teachers with seniority could move. The central district and union would then send a raw recruit to fill such a vacancy. This is how many inner city schools seem to end up with the least experienced teachers.

But I saw that his staff were not raw recruits; most were experienced older men and women.

"How have you managed to do this?" I asked. He explained that he worked very hard to build a team. The teachers helped each other. They worked together to make sure students got the attention they needed. They would even walk the neighborhood to be sure parents came to the school for programs and conferences.

"I do a variety of things to celebrate and honor the team members and their achievements. I do everything I can think of to make my teachers want to stay here to be part of a great team. I try to be as visible, as helpful, as supportive as I can. I don't spend too much time in the office. I listen a lot more than I talk."

He went on. "When I get a raw recruit teacher we give the new person as much help as possible and a chance to perform and to show that they can become a valued member of the team. But if they don't measure up, I have found various ways to encourage them to transfer to another school."

In a very challenging environment, this elementary school principal had focused on building a great team, a team of stars. And that team produced results far beyond anyone's expectations.

1.**Your Example**: As the leader of the organization you have a duty and responsibility to set an example for all the other members of the organization.

If you regularly arrive late and leave early, how can you expect your team to be at work on time and work hard until the last minute of the workday? If you take long breaks or go out for a leisurely lunch, how can you expect your team to be conscientiously working all day long?

Many bosses have used the time clock and other devices to make sure employees worked the hours expected of them, even if the boss didn't. These kinds of controls make sure that employees are at their stations when the work day begins and that they don't leave until the work day ends. But what about the hours in between? Are they productive hours or just time-wasting until it is time to punch out?

If you set the right example and have the right staff, you won't need time clocks and other such devices. Your staff will be members of the team, self-motivated to do the full day's work – and then some.

There are many ways in which you must set an example for the staff.

The way you treat the organization's resources sets an important example. These resources might be Internet connections, the telephone, office supplies, space in the office. If you use these for personal business, don't imagine that no one will know about it. You will be setting an example that others will feel free to follow.

You can surely think of other areas in which you set an example for the team. Set a good example and the team will follow that example.

The values that have been established for the organization must be your values, values you live every day. When your team see you living by the values, your example will be a powerful force.

2.**The walk-around**: The walk-around was covered before, in the chapter on controlling. But it is such an important leadership tool, I want to hit this topic again. You might want to take time to go back to the controlling chapter to re-read the walk-around section.

A good leader gets out of the office frequently to see what the team is doing, especially the front-line team members. The walk-around lets team members see you and recognize that you are interested in what they are doing.

It is important to directly see for yourself. Just reading reports will not give you the information you need to lead a winning team.

You walk around often. You observe, ask, listen. You do not bypass the chain of command. If you see issues, you take them up in private with the appropriate supervisor.

You want to be seen as well as to see. You want to listen and hear. You want to be sure to compliment those team members you know are doing a good job. Compliments produce much more right action than criticisms.

Leaders often find that their desk is piled high with work. They feel they cannot get away from the desk. But staying deskbound cannot build a winning team and a successful organization. Do frequent walk-arounds.

3.**Ask and Listen**: On a walk-around and on other occasions when you are with team members, ask. I like to try to start the conversation going by asking an innocuous question. "How are things going?"... "Are you encountering any problems?"... "Is there anything you need help with?"..."Is anything creating a problem for you?" "What good news have you got?"

Then listen. Listen attentively. Listen carefully, without comment or interruption. While you are listening make mental notes about actions that need to be taken to deal with problems, to take advantage of opportunities, or to improve teamwork.

Unless the item is very minor, do not make out-loud judgments, give orders, or short-circuit the normal chain of command. If the person you are talking to has a supervisor, you want to talk to the supervisor about any matters that you believe need attention.

The supervisor may tell you why these matters are not significant, or the supervisor may explain how these matters are being dealt with. Or the supervisor may bring to your attention a more nuanced or inclusive view of the situation. There may well be matters that you, as the leader, must address.

Ask and listen. Too many people in leadership positions want to tell, to do all the talking. That is a very good way to turn off team members and end up without a winning team. Of course, sometimes you have to give direction and provide feedback. But if you do that before asking and listening you will often be surprised by a negative reaction that impedes rather than accelerates progress. One of the most important leadership tasks is listening.

4.**Be sure everyone knows the mission, the values, the vision, the plan**: Of course, in the training of new staff members you saw to it that they understood the organization's mission. But in the heat of the daily activities, it is easy to forget why the team needs to work so hard. You must to be sure that every member of the team clearly understands what the organization is trying to accomplish, what it seeks to deliver to its customers or clients.

Yes, you told them once, even gave them a card with the mission statement printed on it. But it is too easy to get bogged down in minutia, to be coping with what seem to be unnecessary or even ridiculous demands for time and effort. "Why are we doing this?" is a frequent question by employees who don't know the mission, vision, and plan.

People who clearly understand what they are working for will be much more willing to work hard. And they will be much more willing to lend a hand to another team member who seems bogged down.

I have observed organizations where the employees know only their own small part of the process. They don't understand the big picture – no one has told them how what they do is part of an overall effort aimed at achieving a clearly-defined mission. Because these employees have such a narrow view of their job, they can't deal with unexpected problems. They can't be self-directing because real self-direction requires understanding of the total process of the whole organization.

Work at conveying the mission, values, vision, and plan consistently and often.

5.**Share information regularly on performance vs. budget:** Some leaders want to keep all this data secret. That is a mistake. You need to regularly let your staff know how things are going. For them to be self-directed, they need to know whether operations are going as planned and where there needs to be change to get on track. With a small staff, it is worthwhile to have a brief meeting every period when the results are known. Take questions and answer them as truthfully as you can. Then send the staff off to repeat the success or to improve where improvement is needed. (The chapter on controlling covers this in more detail.)

With a large staff, you still need to let people know how things are going. You need to find effective ways to do this if you can't do it personally. I made this an important task for my supervisors. Each month, after I had gone over results with them, they were expected to assemble their people and go over the results, with an emphasis on how those results affected their particular department. The best supervisors invited their staff to suggest ways to improve the results. (Encouraging innovation is always beneficial.)

If your reports are complicated or if your staff has had little experience with financial and other reports, you need to spend time educating them. You don't want staff leaving a meeting mumbling, " I don't understand what all those numbers mean."

Your team will perform much better if they know and understand the score.

6.**Celebrate the team**: When good things happen, be sure to celebrate and to acknowledge those team members who made the good things happen. Taking some time out of the work routine to celebrate triumphs is well worthwhile and will lead to further team efforts that produce more triumphs.

Celebrate big orders, major new customers, or new contracts. Celebrate new grants or new client groups coming on board. Celebrate key milestones.

There are many ways to do this. A cake at lunch. With a small staff, you could take everybody out to lunch (an inexpensive one.) Throw a party with banners and silly hats. You can think of many, many ways to celebrate the work of the team. What you do is not nearly as important as doing something out of the ordinary to celebrate team triumphs.

Of course, bad things can happen too. They should not be publicly "celebrated." Instead, have a closed-door session with the team members involved. Ask and listen.

Your job is not to rush to blame and censure. Instead, you want to learn why the bad things happened and work with the team members involved to correct the problem and avoid a recurrence.

I have often said in this book that if you have a bad person on the team, you must get rid of that person. If the problem is caused by a person unable or unwilling to be a good team member, then take action.

But usually, problems come about because of outside circumstances, unexpected and unforeseen issues, new threats arising. You need a strong and flexible team to deal with such situations. Playing the blame game, looking for a scapegoat, chewing someone out for a problem they could not control is very counter-productive.

You want the problem solved, the threat averted. A strong team, working together is the best means to achieve this. Degrading a team member won't get the job done.

Let me repeat the first part of this section: celebrate the triumphs of the team. Do it as often as there are triumphs – big or small. When you publicly celebrate the good things your team has accomplished, you will build more team commitment and accomplishments.

In sports, great teams know the score and they celebrate their successes. As a leader, you must see that your staff knows the score and that their successes are celebrated.

WORKING WITH A BOARD

In most organizations, the leader works for a board or with a board. Perhaps the leader is also a board member, or perhaps not. A good leader needs to have a clear understanding of what an effective board does.

What follows is a brief review of the responsibilities of board members. I am indebted to Peter Brinckerhoff for the work he has done in defining what a good board member must do.

Board members are fiduciaries of the organization. A fiduciary has a legal obligation to provide careful oversight of the assets of the organization. Failure to attend to that obligation can put board members at risk of legal action.

Board members must be sure that all legally required tax returns, reports, and other documents are filed on a timely and accurate basis. Board members don't prepare these but they must take positive steps to be sure these have been prepared and submitted as required. The board should have a calendar showing when various reports must be filed. At each board meeting, the board can check to see if the reports due during that period have been filed on a timely basis.

The board needs to be sure that the organization has appropriate insurance as well as plans to deal with emergencies and natural disasters.

Board members need to review and approve the mission statement, the vision, the strategic plan, and the annual budget. In many cases, the leader will work with the board on these thinking tasks, enlisting the board's experience and knowledge. More brains, better outcomes.

Of course, the board should review the actual results against the budget on a regular basis. This might be once a month. If results are not going as planned, then the board needs to be sure the leader is taking the actions needed to get on track. (Some boards meet quarterly. These boards should be provided with monthly reports. Any questions can then be raised with a phone call or email, without waiting until the next scheduled board meeting.)

Board members work with the leader to establish and review critical policies for the organization. Cash control policies are essential. The organization's accountant should be asked to draw up cash control policies for board approval.

Personnel policies are also important and should be developed by the board working with the leader. It may be desirable to engage a personnel/human resources specialist to assist, if there is not such a person on the board.

The board needs to have its own rules, especially concerning conflicts of interest.

The board must be sure that the organization is in compliance with the requirements of major contracts, loans, grants, and so forth. This means the board needs to be sure it has familiarized itself with the requirements of these important relationships.

Board members should be ready to work with the leader to meet with major customers or clients, major funders, large suppliers, community leaders, and so on. Board members need to be ready to be positive representatives for the organization.

The board of directors elects the legally designated officers of the organization.

The board hires, evaluates (and replaces, if necessary) the leader. The leader works for the board.

BUT all of the other employees of the organization work for the leader. Board members should be able to listen to employees to learn more about the operations. But board members should never tell employees what to do. If the board member sees a problem, then the board member should go to the leader. (Micro-managing board members are an all-too-frequent problem.)

Board members usually work with the leader to recruit new board members. New board members need to have training (and enculturation) so that they can be effective as soon as possible.

126

Perhaps the leader or a long-serving board member can take on this task.

Board members should never make promises on behalf of the organization, unless specifically authorized by the whole board to do so.

A good board member comes to the meetings. He or she comes to the meetings prepared, having reviewed any documents sent out in preparation for the meeting. At the meeting a good board member actively participates in discussions and in reaching decisions (while being sure to listen to the views of other board members.)

When a decision is made, the board member supports it, even if he or she spoke against the decision in the meeting. If the decision is totally unacceptable to a board member, then the board member should resign. Public opposition by a board member to a board decision is absolutely inappropriate. (But opposition to an unethical decision or one that does not honor the values of the organization may require a different course of action.).

A good board makes sure the organization has effective leadership, that it is financially sound, that it has taken the necessary steps to meet its fiduciary responsibilities. A good board accepts the risk of possible failure when an action is taken that seems to be good for the organization, but which does not work out. A good board can adapt effectively to change.

And finally, a good board should be composed of members who come from different backgrounds and have experiences and different views. Despite these differences, the members of a good board respect each other and work hard to reach consensus.

I have worked with many boards, of for-profit companies and not-for-profit organizations. Unfortunately, not all boards and board members live up to these expectations.

Sometimes, the board consists of cronies or buddies who look upon the position as a way to gain status and money. They have little interest in the hard work an effective board member should do. This puts much greater responsibility on the leader. The leader must do the organization's leadership tasks as well as work on the board's responsibilities

Sometimes, in a family-owned company, the board consists of family members who are on the board because of their relationship to the family, not because of their knowledge and experience.

A good leader may have to work with a board that is less than ideal. The leader can't really ignore the board, though that is a temptation. After all, the board has legal responsibilities and authority.

The leader must often work diligently to try to educate board members, to help them become more effective and useful. Some of this can be done in board meetings. In my experience, more can be accomplished in one-on-one meetings with board members who need to have a better understanding of what their job requires. Leaders may begrudge the time spent on such activities. But it is a necessary task.

In some organizations, the chairman or president of the board is the real leader of the organization. Perhaps that is your situation. If so, all that has been said about the thinking and doing tasks of leaders will apply to you.

I have found that organizations of size function more effectively when there is a clear separation between the chairman or president of the board and the day-to-day leadership of the organization. Of course, many corporations have a single person who is both the leader of the organization and the head of the board of directors. There is increasing pressure from shareholders and others to separate these two positions. I believe that is wise.

In a very small organization, you may do it all. You can't afford to have a board so you are, in essence, the board as well as the leader. But as your organization grows, you need to move away from this model toward the more usual structure of a board and a leader. For one thing, a good board brings knowledge, experience, and contacts to the organization that the leader may not have or may not have time to exercise. More brains, better outcomes.

There are many resources available on building and maintaining an effective board. I have tried to touch on the highlights and show some of the characteristics of an effective relationship between the board and the leader.

This book is about leadership. In most organizations, the board has a major role to play in leadership. But the board is not the leader. The leader must work with the board, and for the board, utilizing board members as valuable resources to increase the success of the organization.

AXIOMS AND PRINCIPLES FOR EVERY ORGANIZATION LEADER

There various short sayings – axioms, if you will – that I have tried to keep in mind throughout my career. They are the kind of sayings that some leaders post above their desks as reminders. Here are some I have found valuable.

Never be satisfied!

A leader who is satisfied with the organization is a leader who is not looking ahead and seeking out better ways to do things. Satisfaction turns into smugness turns into complacency. And that is when an organization starts to slip.

If you are in a hole, stop digging!

This is similar to the saying, "Don't throw good money after bad." As soon as you know you have a project that is not working, stop it. Get out of the hole, stop throwing more money at it. Many leaders get their egos caught up in losing undertakings. They want to keep on, in the hope there will be "light at the end of the tunnel." But if it is a hole, not a tunnel, swallow your ego and call it quits. You and your staff have much better things to pursue than trying to resuscitate a dead horse.

A related axiom is *Back winners! Bury losers!* It is far better to recognize losers sooner rather than later. We naturally become ego-invested in our projects. This is a well-known human trait. It is emotionally difficult to abandon a losing project. But success won't come from digging the hole deeper. Good leaders know when to quit.

Management is anticipation, not reaction!

Poor managers or leaders spend their time reacting to one crisis after another. Good managers or leaders anticipate what might go wrong and prepare for it. Unforeseen problems will arise. Unexpected accidents will happen. But a solidly-led organization has the flexibility and the procedures to deal with these. If you are not thinking ahead, you are not leading.

Promise only what you can deliver – deliver what you promise!

The quickest way to lose customers or clients is to promise something you can't deliver. The quickest way to lose employee trust is to promise something you can't deliver. Be very cautious with promises when you aren't confident you can meet them. And when you make a promise, do everything in your power to deliver. Unfulfilled promises are a quick way to lose trust. Trust is essential to organizational success.

Leadership combines enthusiasm and objectivity!

If you are not enthusiastic about your organization, about its mission, about its activities, how can you expect anyone else to be enthusiastic? But at the same time, as a leader, you cannot let enthusiasm blind you to reality. You must be objective so that changes can be made when needed. (See *Stop digging...* above.) The combination of enthusiasm and objectivity makes for effective leadership.

No tree grows to the sky!

Nothing grows forever. If your organization has been growing rapidly, or if a product or service has been growing in revenues rapidly, you can be sure that the growth will not continue forever at that pace. In your five-year vision, you need to take into account the likely slowdown of high-growth activities. A caution: sometimes what looks like revenue growth is only inflation. You

131

need to look at non-dollar measures of growth – number of units sold, number of client sessions, or whatever measurement units will give you a non-dollar, non-inflation-affected measure of how growth is going.

You can't save your way to success!

When times get tough and the organization faces financial troubles, the first instinct is to cut costs. That is often the right thing to do to avoid bankruptcy. But in the longer term, cutting costs to save money can only lead to eventual disaster. It is only revenue growth that can make an organization successful over time. If you need to cut costs and save money, you need to also be planning on how to grow revenues.

First, listen and understand – then you can be heard and understood!

Many leaders work hard to make sure that their words are understood by employees, customers, funders, etc. But they often fail. The failure to be understood often comes from the leader's failure to understand. Leaders need to listen first and to ask questions when they do not understand. Understanding the viewpoints of others is a critical part of good leadership. When people see that you have understood them, they will be willing to understand you.

Bad actions produce bad results!

Unethical or immoral activities never succeed in the long-run. The short-term gains from cutting ethical corners always get wiped out by the long-term consequences. If you haven't made this a key value, I encourage you to do so. An ethical organization always has a long-term advantage.

Timing is critical!

Leaders must be highly sensitive to timing. Being either too early or too late leads to failure. Impatient leaders fail often. Procrastinating leaders fail often. Leaders have knowledge or aspirations that make them want to act. But they need to consider what timing will make the action successful. When considering any new project you must ask, "Is the market ready for this? Are we too early to get traction? Or are we too late to be the leader? Or is this the right time for this project?" Right timing makes success easy.

Everything is connected to everything else!

The ecologists repeat this often. It applies to organizations as well. It is not possible to make a change within an organization that does not affect the entire organization. This is especially true in smaller organizations. Think through all of the consequences before acting. It is better to consider the consequences in advance of an action than to have to deal with them after the action has been taken.

No decision is a decision!

It is often tempting to put off a decision until more facts are in. But you will never have all the facts. It is often tempting to hold off on a decision because "the timing isn't right." But the timing may never be exactly right. When you don't make a decision, you have made a decision – a decision to keep on as before. And that no-decision decision may create many more problems than if a decision had actually been made, even without all the facts, even without being sure that the timing was right.

What follows is an important principle for leaders.

Dealing with Conflict:

In every organization there is disagreement and conflict. Disagreement and conflict arise when plans are being considered that affect the future. Because the future is unknowable and the results of plans for the future are uncertain, people will often disagree. Leaders must deal with disagreements and conflicts.

Poor leaders seek to avoid conflict. Conflict within an organization is uncomfortable. Whatever is decided is likely to make someone unhappy.

So poor leaders often put off decisions, hoping that somehow the conflict will go away. (See *"No decision is a decision"* above.) Not making a decision because of not wanting to make anyone unhappy is sure to make everyone unhappy.

Poor leaders often try to make a decision that will satisfy everyone. That usually means the decision is the wrong one. Most correct decisions do not make everyone happy. A decision aimed at universal happiness usually leads to bad outcomes. It almost always leaves everyone less than satisfied.

Organizations get into trouble when the leader tries to avoid conflict and tries to satisfy everyone.

Good leaders anticipate conflict. They follow a process to deal with it. First, they carefully listen to the views of all those concerned with the decision. They do not announce a decision during this process. They listen and gain understanding of the different positions.

Then, taking all of the views they have heard, as well as the views they have developed for themselves, good leaders come to a decision.

(If the decision is very important, it is valuable to have others, such as board members, or outsiders involved with the organization, contribute to the decision process. The more brains, the better the decision. The good leader enlists as many brains as possible and listens carefully.)

When the leader has made a decision, the good leader meets privately with those who will be upset about the decision, tells them of the decision, acknowledges the concerns of those opposed to the decision, and then announces when the decision will be made public.

This step is important to forestall public negativism from those not in agreement with the decision. Sometimes with a very critical decision, in the private meeting the leader must ask those opposed if they will put aside their opposition and work hard to make the leader's decision effective. If the leader cannot get that commitment, it may be that someone will have to leave the organization.

Once a decision is made, it must be implemented as effectively as possible by the people who must work together. Anyone who speaks publicly against the decision will be a very negative influence and must change or go.

Once a decision on a critical issue is publicly announced, then get on with implementation.

It could turn out to have been the wrong decision. Again, deciding what to do in the uncertain future always carries the risk of being wrong. If the decision turns out to be wrong, admit it, and then decide what will be the best course of action to ensure the organization's future success.

But do not put off decisions in order to avoid conflict. It is better to move forward decisively than to try to make everyone happy.

What axioms or principals have you got posted above your desk?

THE END (A Summary)

Congratulations! You have come to the final chapter in this book. I hope that the preceding chapters have given you new insights and new tools with which to become an even more successful leader of a successful organization.

Let me recap and summarize the main ideas this book has put forward.

We began with thinking tasks. Thinking always needs to precede doing.

First came definitions. Defining your organization's products or services was the first, then a definition of your customers or clients, followed by a definition of what your customers or clients want to get from your organization. Core competencies were defined. The final definition asked you to consider your own relationship to the organization.

Many organizations I have worked with have never really defined these matters. They aren't focused. They understand the product or service that appears on the invoice, but that may not be the real product or service that customers or clients want and value.

It seems easy to decide who the organization's customers or clients are. But often the organization has several – users, choosers, payers. Each needs attention.

And all too many organization leaders don't really know what the customer or client wants. They think they know, but when I go with leaders to talk to customers or clients, what we hear is often far different than what was expected.

If you do nothing else after reading this book, be sure you have thought through these definitions.

The definitions need to be sharpened by thinking about awareness, ability to pay, and access. If potential customers don't know about what the organization offers they won't buy its products or services. If they can't afford to pay for the products or services, there will be no transactions. They may know about the organization's products or services. They may be able to afford to pay. But if the potential customers cannot easily access the product or service, no transaction will occur. Thinking about these three factors – awareness, ability to pay, and access – will make the definitions more realistic..

The next thinking task was to encapsulate these definitions into a mission statement that will be made publicly available to anyone involved with your organization. The mission statement will tell what your organization does, who it does it for, and how or why it does it. The mission statement should attract people to your organization; customers or clients, funders, board members, community leaders, and so on. To do this, the mission statement can't be wishy-washy hot air.

Then the key values that the organization should hold to, values that would lead the team to accomplish the mission needed to be articulated and distributed. The values describe how you and you staff will work to accomplish the mission.

Next came the creation of a five-year vision for the organization. What would the organization look like in five years time? What would it be offering, to which customers or clients? How would the organization be changed over the five years? The five-year vision sets a long-range goal.

Serious barriers could arise to keep the vision from happening. Identifying possible barriers to success is a vital thinking task. Developing plans to cope with these barriers, should they occur, is an important leadership responsibility.

To make the vision happen and overcome the possible barriers, a five-year strategic plan must be developed. This includes a cash flow plan and an organizational plan. You learned why a cash flow plan is far more valuable than the usual accrual accounting plan.

From the strategic plan came the annual budget for the first year, a budget more detailed than the plan. Each year, the strategic plan would add a new fifth-year. Each year, the budget would be prepared for the coming year. As the strategic plan and the budget were revised and updated in light of actual events, it might be necessary to revisit the definitions and the mission.

All of this thinking surely gave you and your organization much better focus, and a much greater likelihood of success.

The thinking tasks led to doing tasks. The first doing task is staffing – to ensure that the right people are in place to make the plans happen. I have emphasized several times: having the right people is a very important part of success. This chapter covered job descriptions, recruiting, interviewing, and dealing with hiring mistakes.

Getting the right people might involve finding and engaging outside resources to take on tasks better handled by specialists.

The training of staff members is necessary to make sure they know how to do the job. Training was not a one-time activity. Ongoing coaching is an important task.

And then enculturation was explained. Your staff members need to buy into the culture of your organization in order to succeed. A strong culture builds a strong organization.

Directing is the next doing task. Of course, you and your supervisors will be providing direction to the staff. But the best direction is staff self-direction. Various ways to build staff self-direction were outlined.

Delegation of responsibility and authority is necessary in any organization with more than a handful of employees. Successful delegation is based on trust, with verification that the trust is well-placed.

As the leader you are in control, which means your activities in controlling the operations and results of the organization are critical. A key part of controlling is comparing actual results with planned results and then taking action to deal with discrepancies. The walk-around was discussed and the importance of listening was stressed.

The doing section ended with the great circle – the leadership mandala showing how one task leads to the next task in a great circle.

A very useful analysis tool was presented – SWOT analysis. This is a process to identify the organization's strengths, weaknesses, opportunities, and threats. From the SWOT analysis comes better focus and better results.

A useful process was outlined to do an organizational SWOT analysis.

Then there was a chapter on cost-benefit analysis. Projects and investments need to be analyzed so that you only take on projects and make investment when the expected benefits exceed the costs by enough to justify proceeding. The three factors in this analysis are the costs, the benefits, and the time period over which the analysis will be made. Projecting several possible outcomes, including the worst case, was recommended.

Building a great team is one of the most important functions of a leader. No organization can be really successful without a great team. A variety of ways to build and maintain a great team were suggested. A leader's primary responsibility is getting the right people on the team. The right people produce the right results.

Leaders almost always work with or for a board. This chapter outlined the key responsibilities of the board. Understanding these responsibilities of the board will help the leader to work more effectively with the board.

Then came a series of axioms and principles. These are brief maxims that every leader ought to keep somewhere in his or her head. Even though these appeared toward the end of the book, I hope you spent time thinking about each one. Perhaps this chapter suggested some additional axioms that have been important to you.

And then there is The End, a summary of the ideas and techniques that make up the bulk of this book. You are reading The End now.

And after The End there is the Appendix – Acme Widgets' Cash Flow Budgets for years one through three.

If cash flow is not an easy concept for you, you should have spent time with the cash flow budget prepared for Acme Widgets. A close study of the scenarios and the spreadsheets for these cash flow budgets will be very helpful in doing your own very necessary cash flow budgets.

Finally, you will see Acknowledgments, which suggest some valuable authors for leaders.

I hope that you have gained new ideas and learned valuable techniques and procedures that will make you a better leader.

I hope that this book will help the organization you lead become even more valuable to its employees, to its customers or clients, to its suppliers, to its funders, and to the broader society which all organizations must ultimately serve. Valuable organizations come from good leadership. I hope this book has helped you to become an even better leader.

My best wishes for your success!

ACME WIDGETS CASH FLOW BUDGET

In order to demonstrate the preparation of a cash flow budget we will create a mythical company, Acme Widgets. The cash flow budgets for Acme will cover the first three years of operations. Acme will produce and sell widgets.

To prepare a cash flow budget you need time, imagination, and a calculator. You are predicting the future, always a difficult task. You also may need some assistance. Cash flow budgets are much better if they are developed with a partner or a team so that ideas can be shared (and poor guesses for the future can be shot down.)

The cash flow budgets shown below only show income taxes paid at one time during the year. Many other taxes are ignored for this exercise. But you can't ignore them in real life. Unless taxes are your specialty, you need a tax accountant to provide you with input on the taxes you will likely owe and when you will owe them .

Here is how I have prepared the cash flow budgets that follow. I began by writing a first-draft scenario for the year. The scenario predicted what payments would be received from customers, and when. It predicted when Acme would purchase and pay for machines and for raw materials to convert into finished widgets. Predictions were made in the scenario for payment of rent, office expenses, advertising, and of course, salaries.

The scenario was then transferred to a month-by-month spreadsheet. The row for "Investment" and for "Loan" was blank at first. But as the first year's spreadsheet developed, the amount of capital needed for the operations became clear. I decided that the owners could invest $80,000 and then they could borrow $50,000. They would get that loan for six months and would pay interest only at 8%, repaying the principal at the end of the six months. The spread sheet then showed me that this could be done only with an additional cash infusion from the owners. There was a period during the year when there would not be enough cash.

Then the scenario needed to be revised in light of what the spreadsheet numbers showed. This back and forth between the scenario and the spreadsheet is the way budgeting works.

While these spreadsheets have been developed for a mythical for-profit company, the same process works for not-for-profit organizations. They, too, need to budget cash in and cash out, and decide how much investment will be required, from grants, donations, loans, or other sources.

For any smaller organization, doing a cash flow budget is an exercise that will provide many ongoing benefits.

Acme Widgets – Year One Scenario:

1. In the beginning two investors will put $80,000 into Acme, receiving capital stock. They are the owners and they will also become the first employees.

2. The owners will go the bank (and pledging lots of personal collateral) they will borrow $50,000. This occurs at the end of the first month. Interest is $400 a month, beginning in the second month. This short-term loan must be repaid in the seventh month. No principal payments are required for this short-term loan. When the budget is put onto the spreadsheet, it is obvious that Acme will be in a negative cash position when the loan must be repaid in July. The owners ponder on this and decide they must invest $30,000 more in that month. They hope the budget will show enough cash on hand in December so that they can repay this investment. (Look at the spreadsheet and decide if the repayment can be made.)

3. In the first month, the owners plan to buy a widget machine. The machine costs $40,000. They expect to pay for the machine in the following month when it is delivered.

4. Needing some personal income, the owners plan to pay themselves – $4,000 a month for each – a total of $8,000 a month. These salaries won't be paid until the first few days of the succeeding month. (In the first few days of year two, the salaries for month twelve of year one will be paid.)

5. Acme Widgets needs a home. The owners plan to rent space at $1,000 a month. The rent will need to be paid in advance.

6. Acme Widget will have various office expenses. These are estimated at $200 a month, paid during the month.

7. Acme won't be able to sell widgets unless it advertises. It plans to spend $4,000 in month three, another $4,000 in month six, and another $4,000 in month nine.

8. Acme expects to begin selling widgets in month four, but customers won't pay until the following month. The owners hope and plan for sales during the first year of $292,000. At the end of year one, they expect that customers will owe them $50,000 for sales made in month twelve. For the spreadsheet,

144

they will need to predict customer payments (cash in) for each month.

9. There won't be any widgets to sell unless Acme buys the raw materials to feed into the widget machine. In month two the owners plan to purchase $20,000 of raw materials. But they will pay in the following month. In month four they expect to purchase more raw materials, paying in month five. They expect to pay for $120,000 of raw materials during the first year. The payments need to be spread over the twelve-month period. (Acme will owe another $15,000 in the first month of year two for raw materials purchased in month twelve of year one but not yet paid for.)

You will see how these planned cash flows, in and out, are recorded in the cash flow budget spreadsheet shown on the following page. (The spreadsheet is sideways so you can see all twelve months on a single page.)

CASH FLOW BUDGET FOR ACME WIDGETS

Year One	Jan	Feb	Mar	Apr	May	Jun	Jul	Aug	Sep	Oct	Nov	Dec	TOTAL
Investment	80,000						30,000						110,000
Loan	50,000												50,000
Purchase Machine		40,000											40,000
Purchase Raw Materials			20,000		10,000	10,000	12,000	12,000	13,000	13,000	15,000	15,000	120,000
Pay Rent	1,000	1,000	1,000	1,000	1,000	1,000	1,000	1,000	1,000	1,000	1,000	1,000	12,000
Pay Office Expenses	200	200	200	200	200	200	200	200	200	200	200	200	2,400
Pay Salaries		8,000	8,000	8,000	8,000	8,000	8,000	8,000	8,000	8,000	8,000	8,000	88,000
Advertise			4,000			4,000			4,000				12,000
Loan Interest		400	400	400	400	400	400						2,400
Repay Loan							50,000						50,000
Customer Payments					15,000	18,000	20,000	24,000	32,000	38,000	45,000	50,000	242,000
CASH IN	130,000	0	0	0	15,000	18,000	50,000	24,000	32,000	38,000	45,000	50,000	402,000
CASH OUT	1,200	49,600	33,600	9,600	19,600	23,600	71,600	21,200	26,200	22,200	24,200	24,200	326,800
NET CASH FLOW	128,800	-49,600	-33,600	-9,600	-4,600	-5,600	-21,600	2,800	5,800	15,800	20,800	25,800	75,200
CASH ON HAND	128,800	79,200	45,600	36,000	31,400	25,800	4,200	7,000	12,800	28,600	49,400	75,200	

Acme Widgets – Year Two Scenario:

1. In year two the owners plan to sell $730,000 worth of widgets. They expect to be paid the $50,000 that customers will owe at the end of year one, plus $665,000 for sales paid for in year two. Customers will owe $65,000 at the end of year two.
2. Of course, raw materials will be needed. The owners plan to pay the $15,000 Acme owed for raw materials at the end of year one. Then they expect to pay $323,000 to purchase raw materials during year two. These purchases will be about the same each month. At the end of year two, they plan to owe $33,000 for the raw materials purchased in month twelve but not paid for.
3. In the first month, the owners believe they will have the cash to repay the $30,000 loan they made to Acme in year one.
4. The owners plan to continue paying themselves a total of $8,000 a month, payable in the month following. The plan must include the $8,000 that will be paid in month one of year two for salaries earned in month twelve of year one, and then $8,000 will carry over into year three, when year two December salaries will be paid in the first few days of January of year three.
5. The owners decide they will need help. They plan to hire a machine operator at the beginning of the year. They expect to pay $2,800 a month, paid in the first days of the month following.
6. Office expenses are expected to continue at $200 a month.
7. Acme Widgets plans to continue renting the building for the first six months of the year, at $1,000 per month paid in advance. Then the owners of Acme hope to buy the building. The building owner has talked about selling it to them for $150,000. The Acme owners expect to make a down payment of $50,000. They plan to take on a ten-year mortgage for the remaining $100,000 at 8% interest which would require a monthly payment of $1,214. They will need to work on the spreadsheet to see if they can expect to have enough cash on

hand to make the down payment, or if they will need to invest more.

8. Of course, they must plan for advertising. They anticipate spending $5,000 in each of four different months.

9. Toward the end of the year, Acme plans to purchase a license for a new production process that will significantly increase output. The fee for the license is $6,000.

10. Acme will also have to pay the income taxes it owes for the income in year one. The amount is $3,200. (Of course, there are various other taxes, but for the purposes of this example, we will ignore them.)

11. Finally, the owners hope their cash position will allow for a year-end bonus of $12,000. This goes on the spreadsheet. They also plan for a dividend, a first return on their investment. They hope to be able to pay out $40,000 at the end of year two. Of course, they need to develop the spreadsheet to see if there will be enough cash on hand in December to make such a large payout.

You will see how these amounts are entered into the cash flow budget spreadsheet for year two, shown on the following page. (Remember, the cash on hand at the end of year one is the cash position at the beginning of year two.)

CASH FLOW BUDGET FOR ACME WIDGETS													
Year Two	Jan	Feb	Mar	Apr	May	Jun	Jul	Aug	Sep	Oct	Nov	Dec	TOTAL
Cash on Hand	75,200												
Purchase Raw Materials	15,000	25,000	27,500	27,500	30,000	30,000	30,000	27,500	30,000	30,000	33,000	33,000	338,500
Salaries & Bonus	8,000	10,800	10,800	10,800	10,800	10,800	10,800	10,800	10,800	10,800	10,800	23,800	139,800
Pay Office Expenses	200	200	200	200	200	200	200	200	200	200	200	200	2,400
Advertise	5,000			5,000					5,000			5,000	20,000
Rent	1,000	1,000	1,000	1,000	1,000	1,000	1,000						7,000
Down Payment							50,000						50,000
Payments on Mortgage								1,214	1,214	1,214	1,214	1,214	6,070
Purchase License										6,000			6,000
Income Taxes			3,200										3,200
Repay Owners' Loan	30,000												30,000
Dividend												40,000	40,000
Bonus												12,000	
Customer Payments	50,000	50,000	55,000	55,000	55,000	60,000	60,000	50,000	50,000	60,000	60,000	65,000	670,000
CASH IN	125,200	50,000	55,000	55,000	55,000	60,000	60,000	50,000	50,000	60,000	60,000	65,000	745,200
CASH OUT	-59,200	-37,000	-42,700	-44,500	-42,000	-42,000	-92,000	-39,714	-47,214	-48,214	-45,214	-115,214	-654,970
NET CASH FLOW	66,000	13,000	12,300	10,560	13,000	18,000	-32,000	10,286	2,786	11,786	14,786	-50,214	90,230
CASH ON HAND	66,000	79,000	91,300	101,800	114,800	132,800	100,800	111,086	113,872	125,658	140,444	90,230	

Acme Widgets – Year Three Scenario:

1. Salaries for the owners ($8,000 a month) and for the machine operator ($2,800 a month) are expected to continue in year three. But the owners of Acme Widgets plan to go into the fluted widget business, a new product line. A fluted widget machine operator will be hired at $3,000 per month. They plan to begin paying that salary in month four.
2. A fluted widget machine is planned for. The machine will cost $72,000 and the machine maker expects cash on delivery in month three. The owners need to be sure that cash will be available to make such a large payment. (Will more investment be needed?)
3. Advertising for regular widgets is planned at $24,000 for the year, spaced out as before. But if fluted widgets are to be sold, these must have advertising, too. To get the line launched, the owners plan to spend $12,000 in month four, with three additional ad campaigns at $6,000 each.
4. The owners having been using hand-me-downs and equipment brought from home. They decide they should plan on buying office furniture and equipment. They expect to spend $4,000 as the year begins.
5. Office expenses are expected to increase, to $250 a month and then to $300 a month.
6. The mortgage payments on the building will need to be made. The payment will be $1,214 per month, principal and interest.
7. Of course, the major source of cash coming in to the business is customer payments for regular and fluted widgets. The owners plan on payments during the year for sales of regular widgets totaling $854,000. Then the sales of fluted widgets should get going in May, with payments from customers starting in June. Fluted widget sales are budgeted at $122,000 for the year, with sales starting small and growing throughout the year.
8. And then raw materials will need to be purchased to produce regular and fluted widgets. The owners expect to spend

$431,000 buying raw materials for regular widgets, and $82,000 buying raw materials for fluted widgets.

9. They must pay taxes on the income earned in year two. Their tax accountant tells them to expect to owe $61,860 in March. (To simplify, we will ignore the estimated tax payments that would have to be made.) March will be a tough month with both the tax payment and the payment for the fluted widget machine due. Will there be enough cash? Should they postpone purchase of the fluted widget machine. Look at the cash flow budget spreadsheet and make your decision.

10. The owners look at the cash flow they have budgeted through November to decide if they can pay bonuses and a dividend. They would like to budget $16,000 for bonuses and $24,000 for dividends. What do you think?

The cash flow budget for year three is shown on the next page.

CASH FLOW BUDGET FOR ACME WIDGETS

Year Three	Jan	Feb	Mar	Apr	May	Jun	Jul	Aug	Sep	Oct	Nov	Dec	TOTAL
Cash on Hand	90,230												
Purchase Raw Mtls. Reg.	33,000	33,000	35,000	35,000	36,000	37,000	37,000	35,000	37,000	37,000	38,000	38,000	431,000
Purchase Raw Mtls. Fluted				5,000	5,000	6,000	7,500	10,000	10,500	12,000	13,000	13,000	82,000
Purchase Fluted Widget Machine			72,000										72,000
Salaries & Bonus	10,800	10,800	10,800	13,800	13,800	13,800	13,800	13,800	13,800	13,800	13,800	29,800	172,600
Payments on Mortgage	1,214	1,214	1,214	1,214	1,214	1,214	1,214	1,214	1,214	1,214	1,214	1,214	14,568
Pay Office Expenses	250	250	250	250	300	300	300	300	300	300	300	300	3,400
Advertise - Regular		6,000			6,000			6,000			6,000		24,000
Advertise - Fluted				12,000		6,000				6,000		6,000	30,000
Buy Office Furniture	4,000												4,000
Tax Payment			61,680										61,680
Dividend												24,000	24,000
Customer Payments - Reg	65,000	65,000	70,000	70,000	72,000	73,000	73,000	70,000	72,000	74,000	75,000	75,000	854,000
Customer Payments - Fluted						9,500	11,500	14,000	19,000	21,000	23,000	24,000	122,000
CASH IN	155,230	65,000	70,000	70,000	72,000	82,500	84,500	84,000	91,000	95,000	98,000	99,000	1,066,230
CASH OUT	-49,264	-51,264	-180,944	-67,264	-62,314	-64,314	-59,814	-66,314	-62,814	-70,314	-72,314	-112,314	-919,248
NET CASH FLOW	105,966	13,736	-110,944	2,736	9,686	18,186	24,686	17,686	28,186	24,686	25,686	-13,314	146,982
CASH ON HAND	105,966	119,702	8,758	11,494	21,180	39,366	64,052	81,738	109,924	134,610	160,296	146,982	146,982

152

These cash flow budgets will become increasingly complex as the business grows in size. Years four and five will become more difficult to predict as there are likely to be unexpected factors affecting the operations. But it is still important and valuable to make those farther-out budgets. At least you will know whether or not the five-year vision for the organization has a good chance of being realized. (Of course, you would revise the cash flow budgets annually so there is a new set of five-year budgets each year.)

With larger organizations, preparing cash flow budgets will be neither an easy nor quick task. But it is essential to ensure that the organization can expect to generate sufficient cash flow to be successful. It can be fatal to an organization to run out of cash with no quick way to meet salaries, supplier bills, taxes owed, and so on.

Businesses can have great sales and seem very successful. But if customers pay slowly, if expenditures get too high, a business can run out of cash, even when its sales are going just fine.

(It took me about eight total hours over several days to prepare these scenarios and spreadsheets for Acme Widgets. That will give you an idea of the time requirements for this essential task. Lots of time = lots of benefits.)

A great many organizations prepare budgets using accrual accounting figures. Let me repeat again why that can be a problem.

When Acme Widgets ships out an order of widgets, that shipment is recorded as a sale for accrual accounting purposes – EVEN THOUGH the customer has not paid, may not pay for 60 or more days, or may never pay. Acme Widgets cannot spend money that shows up on its accounting report as sales. It only has real money when customers pay.

When Acme Widgets receives an order of raw materials, that is recorded on the accounting report as an expense – EVEN THOUGH Acme has not paid for the raw materials. When the actual payment is made, cash will go out.

Depreciation and amortization are additional accounting concepts that keep accrual accounting reports from actually showing cash flow.

A budget prepared using the accrual accounting report format may indicate excellent sales, but it won't take into account when customers will actually pay for those sales – when actual money will be available.

This is why I believe it is very important to do cash flow budgeting (and then cash flow reporting.) In a small organization, it is the cash coming in and the cash going out that are the critical factors to plan for and then to watch carefully. Running out of cash often means the demise of the organization.

ACKNOWLEDGEMENTS

This book does not have a bibliography. If you are interested in reading more about leadership and management, you will find thousands of books on these subjects. They cover every conceivable aspect of these topics. Some are useful, some are not.

I have found a few authors to be very helpful to me. I have drawn upon their works to make my leadership activities and this book far better. I recommend these authors to any leader.

When I first began to have management responsibility many years ago, I was steered to the works of <u>Peter Drucker</u>. He is one of the most insightful and valuable writers on management and leadership. Drucker has been dead for some years now, but his books remain available. Their wisdom is timeless. I recommend *Managing for Results.* But many other Drucker books and articles will provide wise counsel.

I have worked with <u>Peter Brinckerhoff</u> for many years. He is a leading consultant to not-for-profit organizations and an author whose books have provided practical, example-based guidance to leaders of these organizations. His advice is just as useful to for-profit organizations. *Mission-Based Management* has won awards, gone through many editions, and has helped many leaders. *Smart Stewardship for Nonprofits* is filled with valuable ideas.

<u>Jim Collins</u> is the author of *From Good to Great, Great by Choice,* and many other books. His work, based on extensive research, provides wise guidance to anyone concerned with organizational success. While much of the focus is on larger organizations, any organization leader can learn much from these books.

<u>Daniel Kahneman</u> is a psychologist who won a Nobel Prize in Economics. I came upon his book *Thinking, Fast and Slow* while I was writing this book. Kahneman provides great insight

into how we think, especially how we make decisions. Leaders need to be aware of how easy it is for the unconscious part of the brain to produce poor decisions. Kahneman's work has influenced this book as it should influence your understanding of how humans (including you) think.

A number of people read the drafts of this book and made very helpful comments and criticisms. I have added, revised, deleted, and greatly improved the book because of their help. (But of course, they bear no responsibility for the errors, omissions, fuzzy ideas, or poor wording. Those are my responsibility.)

Jack Taylor has worked with many small businesses. He provided very helpful criticisms and suggestions.

I imposed upon my friendship with Peter Brinckerhoff and asked for his thoughts. He responded with many very helpful criticisms and suggestions.

Members of my family have been deeply involved in entrepreneurial businesses and in leading not-for-profit organizations. I have benefited greatly from their comments and criticisms. Fortunately, the family relationship did not lead them to hold their fire. They will see that the book reflects most of their suggestions for improvement.

The last word. You can make a difference for future leaders. They can benefit from your experiences, both good and bad. As I have tried to pass on what I have learned to help you, I hope you will make an effort to pass on what you have learned in your career so the leaders of tomorrow will be even more successful. Society depends upon wise and effective leadership of its organizations. Each of us can try to pass on what we have learned to ensure wise and effective leadership, leadership that makes our country and our world a better place.

Thank you and my best wishes for your success.

www.ingramcontent.com/pod-product-compliance
Lightning Source LLC
Chambersburg PA
CBHW060605200326

41521CB00007B/673